22 YEARS IN 17 MINUTES

WRITTEN BY

DONALD O. WARE

ISBN: 9798312119923 (Paperback)

Front cover image & Book designed by Joyner Publishing.
Printed in the United States of America.
First printing edition 2023

All statistical facts of "Did You Know?" are provided and rendered by Chatgpt.
https://en.wikipedia.org/wiki/List_of_mass_shootings_in_the_United_States_in_2024?utm_source=chatgpt.com

Joyner Publishing
Tampa, FL, 33547
www.joynerpublishing.com
services@joynerpublishing.com

CONTENTS

In memory of
Aron Trayvon Snordon

FOREWORD

Elder Donald O. Ware, Is a man of God, who loves the Lord with all his heart. He is dedicated to Ministering the Word of God wherever he goes, and to whoever the Lord places in his path. Elder Ware is a father that knows all too well about life and it's hard knocks. Being a single father, and navigating to be the best at it, had its challenges. Donald has weathered the storms, trials and tribulations of fatherhood. I have seen his dedication and resilience to his relationship with his son, before his untimely death. 22 years in 17 minutes gives you a closer, much deeper look into the heart and relationship of Donald and Aron. Evangelist Valerie J. Ware Wife of Elder Donald O. Ware and Momma V to my son in love Aron T. Snordon.

Valerie J. Ware

DEDICATION

This book is dedicated to the life and memory of Aron Trayvon Snordon. I was inspired by God to write this book and to share my testimony to help others understand God's purpose in our lives and that he allows circumstances and situations to come into our lives. For example, some problems do occur to warn us and to help motivate others to lead them in the right direction so they can make the right choices in life.

I dedicate this book to those who have experienced the same loss or the loss of a close loved one to violence in our communities and to let them know that God is in control.

"And we know [with great confidence] that God [who is deeply concerned about us] causes all things to work together [as a plan] for good for those who love God, to those who are called according to His plan and purpose."

- *Romans 8:28 KJV*

ACKNOWLEDGEMENTS

Growing up in Louisville, Ky As a kid was a challenge for me being around gangs, drugs, alcohol, and the city streets, until one day God opened my eyes. God saved me, sanctified me, and filled me with His precious Gift of the Holy Ghost at the age of 22. For that, I give him all the honor, the Glory, and the praise. I would like to acknowledge all those who were there for me and my son through it all. My mother Mary Patterson, went to be with the Lord on June 24, 2022. Mom, you were always there for me and my son. Thank you for watching Aron, while I worked, and for your love and support. I love you, and I miss you so much. My siblings, my brother Michael Ware (The fun brother). My brother Eric Ware was also called home to be with the Lord in 2015. You would watch Aron too, and give me the report if my son has been acting up, or behaving.

One of my Oldest Brothers (Uncle) Alphonso Ware (Sonny) looked out for Aron. You were fun too, and would play games with him growing up, and cooked for my son when he was hungry. My sisters (Aron's favorite aunties Tracy Ware & Lisa Ware) You all spoiled Aron with loving care. My sister Lisa and my son share the same birth date February 11th. My younger brother Leon Ware was one of his favorite uncles. Leon was very overprotective of him growing up, they shared a special bond. My other younger brother Aris Morris was very supportive of Aron's sports. Aris would put money in Aron's pocket with his own LLC account. (Uncle) Jeremy his Mother's Brother always in any way shows his Love & Support to his nephew and to Aron's Godfather and Uncle and his wife's Godmother, Auntie. They were very supportive of Aron, and me too. Anytime we needed something, they came through.

To all of Aron's cousins who grew up with him Dominique, Nisha, Misha, Shoe, Nick, Quinn, Little Eric, Detrick, Tasha, Dashia, Lil Sonny, Tomisha, Rhonda, Latrice, Treshanda, Nicola, Asia, Keith, Keisha. To Macha Snordon, thank you for letting me have full custody. Of Aron, and giving me the opportunity to raise him. For that I am grateful. Our former church family Bible Way Church Of God In Christ, and The 4th Ecclesiastical Indiana North Central Jurisdiction, thank you for all the prayers, support, and love In the time of our crisis, concerning Aron. Yes, Bro. Jacque Morris now Pastor Morris Thank you and your Family for accepting us as Family me & my Son in 2009 in our time of Crisis when we had nowhere to live how God touch your heart and ask your Grandfather Deacon Morris (Who now gone to be with the Lord) for us to stay with yall Temporary until God Bless us and God so I truly thank you.

And also to the California Jets organization President Tammy Hawkins for your support and love in our time of need. To Elder Benjamin Bluitt and his wife Audrey Bluitt, for being there, when we needed you all most. And last but not least my Beautiful Wife Valerie J. Ware for the love she poured into our son and all the times she prayed for him. Spending time with him; was a Beautiful Mother -in-love and Son-in-love Bond they shared. And to our very sweet Daughter Daj'zah who was very close to her brother, who was very supportive and always there for him. To all his Brothers & Sisters Maurice, Erica, Lastaycia, and Markecia, for all the Love and support. *Thank you*

INTRODUCTION

Gun violence has become a familiar and devastating occurrence in our society, leaving behind a trail of unimaginable tragedies. From mass shootings to individual acts of violence, the impact of gun-related incidents extends far beyond the immediate victims. This article aims to delve into the profound consequences of gun violence, shedding light on the human toll and the lasting scars it leaves on individuals, families, and communities.

Lives are cut short. The most heart-wrenching aspect of gun violence is the loss of precious lives. Every victim, be it in a mass shooting or an isolated incident, represents a vibrant human being with dreams, aspirations, and loved ones. Their untimely deaths rob families and friends of their presence, leaving a void that can never be filled.

The tragedies that unfold as a result of gun violence are a painful reminder of the fragility of life. Survivors of gun violence often endure profound physical and emotional trauma. Gunshot wounds can cause severe injuries, leaving lasting disabilities and requiring extensive medical care. The physical recovery is arduous and can have a long-lasting impact on a survivor's quality of life. Additionally, the emotional scars from such traumatic events can manifest as post-traumatic stress disorder (PTSD), anxiety, depression, and survivor's guilt, affecting individuals long after the immediate incident.

It causes ripple effects on families and communities. When gun violence strikes, its impact reverberates far beyond the immediate victims. Families are shattered, forever altered by the loss of a loved one or the burden of caring for a survivor. The ripple effects are felt in communities where fear and a sense of vulnerability can prevail. Witnessing or experiencing gun violence erodes the social fabric, leading to mistrust, isolation, and a diminished sense of safety among community members.

The psychological toll of gun violence cannot be understated. Witnessing or surviving a violent incident can result in long-lasting psychological consequences. Individuals may struggle with anxiety, depression, and fear, making it challenging to resume normal daily activities. The psychological scars can inhibit personal growth, strain relationships, and impede the healing process for years to come. Gun violence has a devastating effect and impact on children and youth.

Experiencing or witnessing violence at a young age can shape their perception of the world, leading to increased levels of fear, anxiety, and aggression come. Gun violence has a devastating effect and impact on children and youth. Experiencing or witnessing violence at a young age can shape their perception of the world, leading to increased levels of fear, anxiety, and aggression.

Traumatized children may struggle academically, socially, and emotionally, hindering their future prospects. The cycle of violence can persist as these young individuals become more vulnerable to negative influences and resort to violence themselves.

Gun violence leaves an indelible mark on individuals, families, and communities, exacting an immeasurable toll on our society. The tragedies born out of gun-related incidents extend beyond the loss of lives; they leave physical and emotional scars that can endure for a lifetime. The ripple effects permeate through families, communities, and the healthcare system, perpetuating a cycle of pain and trauma. Addressing the issue of gun violence requires a collective effort that goes beyond mere rhetoric. It demands comprehensive gun control measures, improved access to mental health services, community engagement, and the cultivation of a culture of non-violence. By acknowledging the devastating consequences of gun violence and working towards effective solutions.

In this book, we will explore the story of my son, Aron, and the life he lived. I pray that this book inspire your to change your direction if you are on the wrong path. I hope that it encourages those on the right path to go out and motivate others to do the same. Above all, I wish that you come to God and receive his goodness.

This is the life of Aron Trayvon Snordon

CHAPTER 1
THE BEGINNING

"Proverbs 22:6 Train up a child in the way he should go [teaching him to speak God's wisdom and will for his abilities and talents], Even when he is old he will not depart from it."

The Life & Story of Aron Trayvon Snordon (February 11, 1999 - August 22, 2021)

Aron Trayvon Snordon was born in Louisville, Ky, at the University of Louisville Hospital on February 11th, 1999, at 2 am in the morning, (8 lb and 12 oz); a healthy child. I was an excited and proud father. When I held him for the first time, it felt so surreal in my mind. I said, "I cannot believe I'm a father and have a son." My only child! I pretty much lived in the hospital for days. Holding him and feeding him made me the happiest man in the world.

It was priceless. At this time, his mother and I were not together. She had broken up with me during the pregnancy. Six months before his birth, as young parents of our first child, I was faced with a challenging choice, and that was abortion.

Not living for God at this time of my life, I felt in my heart not to, so my response was, "No! We laid together, so we will raise this child together." So, as a result of my decision not to abort, with disappointment and anger, she felt led to break up with me. We departed and went our separate ways.

In the early months of her pregnancy, that was when we found out that the baby was a boy. As sad and hurtful as I was then, I continued to buy "baby boy things," like baby clothes, a bed, sleepers, etc. During this time, my heart was broken. One day, my best friend looked at me and saw the disappointment, sadness, and heartbreak on my face. He looked at me and asked, "Do you want to meet someone I have in mind? She may like you!" So in my mind, I told myself, well, it won't hurt me to meet someone. So I answered, "Ok! Cool. Why not!" So we met, became friends, and we started dating.

On February 11th, 1999, I found someone new. My son's mother had moved on with someone else. He was also there at the University of Louisville Hospital. His mother and I had been broken up for six months by the time of his birth. After my son's birth, I ask myself, "Do I want to continue living this life without Christ? And face the huge risk of me getting killed in the streets? Or go to prison and spend most of my life behind a jail cell, not knowing my son?"

I decided to return to church, gave my life to the Lord at Greater Freeborn Baptist Church, and dedicated my son to the Lord by getting him Christening. So here I am, living for the Lord and dedicating my son back to the Lord. However, with every path will come challenges. I had difficulties with working, trying to keep a relationship, and being a full-time father all at the same time was pretty hard. But God was keeping me and helping me and giving me an understanding of how to be a father.

God would send help through people like my mother and sisters so that I could get some rest. So this continued until I got us a apartment.

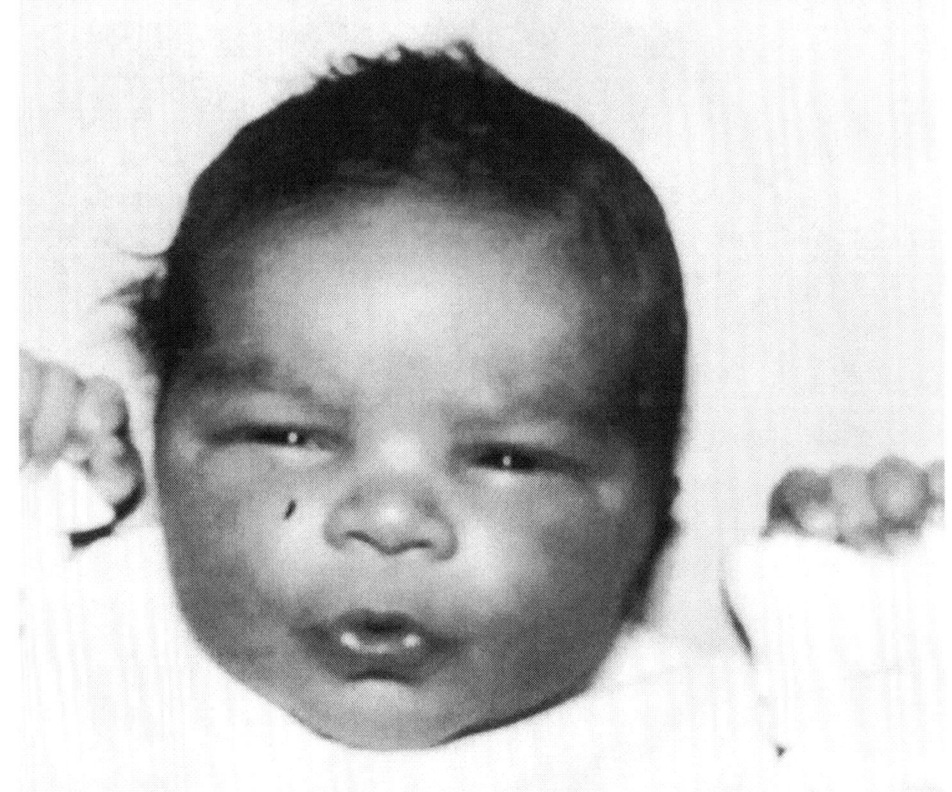
Snordon
8 Lbs. 12 Oz.

DID YOU KNOW?

The effects of gun violence on infants and young children are severe and frequently catastrophic. Even though these young kids might not fully comprehend what happened, there may be short-term, long-term, and psychological as well as physical repercussions.

1. Physical Harm

- Injury or Death: Children under the age of three are particularly susceptible to bodily harm from gunshots. Unintentional shootings are a serious risk in households when firearms are not kept in a safe location.
- Long-term Health Problems: If a kid is hurt but survives, they can have physical or brain injuries that cause developmental delays, persistent pain, or lifelong impairments.

2. Psychological and Emotional Impact

- Trauma Exposure: Even if a young child is not directly harmed, witnessing gun violence or experiencing the aftermath (e.g., seeing a loved one injured or killed) can cause psychological trauma. This may lead to issues like nightmares, anxiety, or PTSD later in life.

- Attachment Disruption: Babies and toddlers rely on caregivers for emotional stability and security. When a parent or close family member is a victim of gun violence, the child's sense of safety and attachment can be severely affected, potentially leading to emotional withdrawal or behavioral issues.

3. Impact on Development

- Cognitive and Behavioral Delays: Children exposed to gun violence may have trouble concentrating, learning, or managing their emotions. Early childhood trauma is linked to difficulties in school readiness and behavioral issues as they grow older.
- Aggressive Behavior: Children who grow up in environments where violence is common may be more likely to exhibit aggressive behaviors themselves as they mimic what they've witnessed, even if they don't fully comprehend it.

4. Family and Community Consequences

- Parental Grief and Stress: Parents and caregivers who lose a child or experience gun violence may become overwhelmed with grief, depression, or anxiety, which can make it harder for them to care for the surviving children in the household.
- Community Impact: Gun violence in neighborhoods can create a pervasive sense of fear and insecurity for families with young children. Lack of access to safe spaces to play and grow can restrict a child's healthy development.

5. Indirect Effects

- Economic Hardship: If a primary breadwinner or caregiver is killed or injured, it can lead to financial difficulties, which may affect the child's access to healthcare, nutrition, and stable housing.

- Displacement: Gun violence may force families to relocate, disrupting routines, social bonds, and access to early childhood services, which are crucial during these formative years.
- The ripple effects of gun violence extend far beyond the immediate moment, affecting the emotional and psychological health of the youngest members of society.

CHAPTER 2
THE CHALLENGE

Train up a child in the way he should go [teaching him to seek God's wisdom and will for his abilities and talents], Even when he is old he will not depart from it.
Proverbs 22:6

"Proverbs 22:6 should not be understood as a promise that Christian children will make good decisions their entire lives. No, it should be understood as a warning. If parents don't discipline their children in a wise way, then their kids are going to make foolish choices and continue to do so when they grow up."

From 1999 to 2004 there were some challenging times in my son's life, at a young age from eight months old to five years old being a child living across the bridge. In New Albany, Indiana my son was living in two different worlds. One was a non-spiritual home and the other was spiritual. At this time he was being exposed to things as far as curse words and verbal abuse living in a household with an Auntie, Uncle, and Cousins was pretty tough for a little toddler who don't know right from wrong. At this time I had joint custody.

I would come and get him every other weekend. During the week I would visit him when I had time when he needed things like pampers, etc.

It was pretty tough at this point in time being married and keeping up with my responsibilities as a father. But God was helping me through it all and he also placed a very special person in my son's life and that was his Grandmother. His mother's mom, God used her to teach my son the Word of God in the midst of all the chaos and madness that was going on in the household where he was living. She would teach him songs like "Jesus on Cavalry," and "The Blood of Jesus" children's spiritual songs.

There was a time when he was about two or three years old when he cursed at his mother and his Grandmother called me immediately. That was the first time I gave my child a whooping. Lesson learned! After that whooping, he never said that again. Now there was a time where his mom would send him to different types of places where I could not find him like close friends of the family houses that I didn't know of and to his godparents who lived in Lexington, Kentucky. I was so upset and very angry at that time but I thank God for his Grandmother. God really used her to help me with these types of situations to find my son. She would give me locations to find him. I had no idea or clue where he would be so his Grandmother would give me direction so I would be on my way to get him at certain locations.

Sometimes there would be difficulties in the communication between me and the godparents, arguments yelling, and screaming threats. I prayed and asked God for guidance and He gave me the courage to go get my child. On one particular time, I didn't understand what was going on because when I arrived there with my little brother & one of my good friends, who grew up with my son, almost did not recognize me because family members and friends would tell my son lies and send him different types of places that almost confused him at a young age that I was not the father.

The Lord brought peace into the situation and my son began to be receptive to me, despite all confusion. During this time in my marriage, it was a challenging time between me and my then-wife. My ex-wife and my son's mother did not like each other due to personal feelings. This tension and feud went on for years.

One Day in 2004 a year after my father passed, sometime in the spring months I received the phone call from my son's mother she said, "I want our son to live with you. I cannot care for him. He is getting out of hand here and you can raise him to be a better man than I can and you can teach him about God."

At this point in my life, I was saved so I replied, "Yes, of course! I would do so but don't we have to take it to court?"

She replied no they do not have to know. We are the parents! It's our decision, not theirs."

I agreed to take Aron at five years old and he was in School, Head Start. I was now a full-time dad and still paying child support because I didn't want her to pay. I continued paying it so his mother could get back on her feet. So now I enrolled him in Frazier Elementary School in Louisville, Kentucky in the fall of 2004.

This Picture was when Aron first start living with me at the age of 5 yrs old He was in kindergarten we was on our way to Church.

DID YOU KNOW?

Gun violence in St. Louis is a significant issue, reflecting broader trends in urban crime and socio-economic challenges. The city has historically faced high rates of gun-related homicides, particularly in certain neighborhoods. Key factors contributing to gun violence in St. Louis include:

1. Concentration in Specific Areas

- Gun violence is often concentrated in neighborhoods with high poverty rates, limited access to education, and economic opportunities.
- Certain parts of North St. Louis, for example, experience disproportionate levels of violence compared to other areas.

2. Social and Economic Inequalities

- St. Louis has a history of racial and economic segregation, which continues to shape its urban landscape.
- Disinvestment in specific communities leads to cycles of poverty and crime.

3. Youth Involvement and Gangs

- A significant proportion of gun violence involves young people, either as perpetrators or victims.

- Gang activity and disputes over illegal activities often escalate into violence.

4. Access to Firearms

- Missouri has relatively lenient gun laws, which makes firearms more accessible.
- The ease of obtaining illegal firearms contributes to the high number of shootings.

5. Community Initiatives

- Efforts such as "Cure Violence" and local community-based programs aim to mediate conflicts and reduce shootings.
- Some grassroots organizations focus on addressing the root causes of violence through education, employment, and mentorship.

6. Law Enforcement Strategies

- The St. Louis Metropolitan Police Department has implemented various strategies, such as hotspot policing and partnerships with federal agencies.
- However, trust between police and communities remains a challenge.

Statistics and Trends:

- St. Louis frequently ranks among cities with the highest per capita murder rates in the United States.
- While overall crime rates may fluctuate, gun-related incidents, especially homicides, remain a persistent concern.

Solutions and Advocacy:

- Efforts to reduce gun violence require a multifaceted approach, including:

- Addressing systemic inequality and improving economic opportunities.
- Strengthening community-police relationships.
- Implementing stricter regulations on firearm sales and ownership.
- Expanding mental health and conflict resolution resources.

If you're interested in specific data, local initiatives, or ways to contribute, let me know!

CHAPTER 3
THE GREAT SEPARATION

And if a house is divided against itself, that house cannot stand. And if Satan has risen up against himself and is divided, he cannot stand, but is coming to an end. But no one can go into a strong man's house and steal his property unless he first overpowers and ties up the strong man, and then he will ransack and rob his house.
Mark 3:25-27

"When you use the expression 'A House Divided Against Itself Cannot Stand', it literally means that success comes from sticking together and to do anything else is to invoke disaster. Example of use: "I wish Ben and Jerry would learn to get along. After all, a house divided against itself cannot stand."

In the year 2003 in April, my Father (his Grandfather) passed away a year before my Son lived with me but I thank God that my Father was able to see his Grandson before he passed when my son was a baby. My son moved in with us in 2004 at 5 years old and started school at Frazier Elementary. In the fall in Louisville Kentucky my son was doing good but started getting into a little trouble at school, and I had to discipline him. Although he was meeting new friends and learning new things at school, I was noticing his attention span.

His condition, "Attention-deficit/hyperactivity disorder" (ADHD) was causing problems and disruptions in the classroom so I decided to get him into football. I began riding around in the city going to city parks to find a team for him to join. He ended up joining a team called "Shawnee Jaguars." At this time, my son was 6 years old; the last year for the age group of flag football before it turned into Mighty Mites in the year 2005. That year is when I began to Coach Football for the Junior Division (10 and 11-year-olds), my son scored his first flag football touchdown against the California Jets where the team won 7-0 and that is when it all began for my son in sports.

This brings back memories of myself when I played Semi-Pro Football when my son was a baby. I played in the Semi-Pro Football League for two seasons with the Louisville Galaxies & Louisville Chargers 2001 - 2003. One season I played cornerback and the second season I played slot receiver and played on the special teams. I saw great potential in my son and decided to put him into football; he was easy to coach and it would help him balance out his energy during the years of 2005 - 2009, during which he played for three city teams Shawnee Jaguars, Iroquois Raiders, and the Shawnee Eagles. Although I became more interested in coaching football, and things were getting better for my son at school and playing sports another problem was rising. My marriage at that time was getting rocky.

Personal problems where it had taken a fall like they say "If the devil chops the head off the body is no good" So around these times I was allowing the devil to get into my marriage causing us to have a lot of disagreements & verbal arguments. I had stopped going to church because of the up-rising problem surrounding the church at that time it was hard to seek spiritual counseling, yes I had backslide from attending church. During this particular time, it was affecting my son as he witnessed two people splitting. She would say things like "You need to be with someone else", etc. Towards the end of 2008 (Barack Obama won the election being the 1st black President of the United States of America at this historical time) she had moved out and separated from us. My son Aron was 9 years old and was in the 4th Grade when she separated from us. She filed for a divorce in May of 2009.

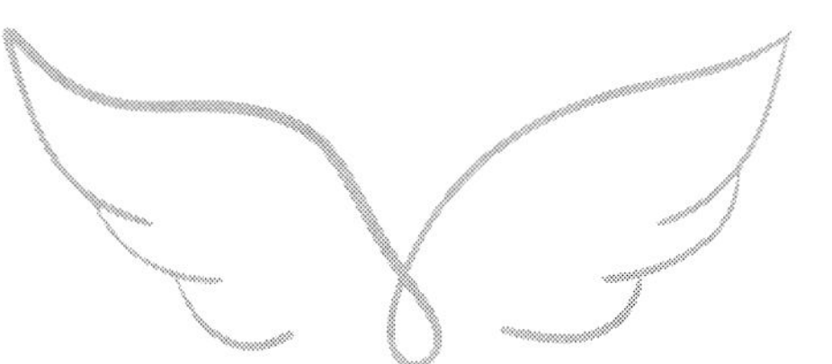

DID YOU KNOW?

Gun violence is a significant concern in Louisville, Kentucky, with patterns that reflect national trends and unique local factors. Similar to other urban centers, Louisville faces challenges related to socio-economic disparities, community disinvestment, and access to firearms. Below are some key aspects of gun violence in Louisville:

1. Concentration of Violence in Certain Areas

- Gun violence in Louisville is often concentrated in neighborhoods with high poverty rates and limited access to resources.
- West Louisville, in particular, has been disproportionately affected, with higher rates of shootings and homicides compared to other parts of the city.

2. Youth and Gang Involvement

- A significant portion of gun-related incidents involves young people, often connected to gang activity or interpersonal conflicts.
- The cycle of violence is fueled by retaliatory shootings, where one incident leads to another.

3. Rising Homicide Rates

- Louisville has seen fluctuations in homicide rates over the years, but recent trends have shown alarming increases in gun-related deaths.
- In 2021, Louisville recorded its highest number of homicides, the majority involving firearms.

4. Contributing Factors

- Economic Inequality: Economic disparities and lack of opportunities create environments where violence becomes more prevalent.
- Historical Segregation: Long-standing racial and economic segregation in Louisville has concentrated poverty and crime in specific areas.
- Access to Firearms: Kentucky's permissive gun laws make it relatively easy for individuals to acquire firearms, contributing to gun-related incidents.

5. Community and Law Enforcement Efforts

- Violence Prevention Initiatives: Programs like "The Office for Safe and Healthy Neighborhoods" focus on violence interruption and community engagement.
- Intervention Strategies: Grassroots organizations work to mediate conflicts and provide resources for at-risk individuals.
- Police Efforts: The Louisville Metro Police Department (LMPD) has increased patrols in high-crime areas and collaborates with federal agencies to target illegal gun trafficking.

6. Public Health and Advocacy

- Community leaders and activists have framed gun violence as a public health crisis, calling for comprehensive approaches that address root causes like poverty, education, and mental health.
- Advocacy groups push for stronger gun control measures and increased funding for violence prevention programs.

Statistics and Current Trends

- Gun-related homicides and non-fatal shootings remain a persistent problem, with many victims being young, Black males.
- Despite efforts to curb violence, Louisville continues to struggle with high gun crime rates relative to its population size.

Solutions and Collaboration

- Addressing gun violence in Louisville requires a combination of systemic change and localized efforts:
    - Economic Investment: Revitalize neglected communities to create jobs and opportunities.
    - Education and Mentorship: Offer programs that provide youth with alternatives to violence.
    - Stronger Firearm Regulations: Advocate for policies to limit access to guns for those at risk of committing violence.
    - Community Engagement: Foster trust between law enforcement and residents to improve cooperation and safety.

If you're looking for detailed data, specific initiatives, or ways to get involved in reducing gun violence in Louisville, I can provide more tailored information.

CHAPTER 4

OUR JOURNEY IN A DARK TIME

Psalms 46:1 "God is our refuge and strength [mighty and impenetrable], A very present and well-proved help in trouble."

"Psalm 46 is a strong biblical passage that reminds us that even in the face of trouble, God is our refuge and strength." "I talked about the fact that the bible doesn't talk about the absence of calamity, but God promises his presence in trying times.

In the years 2009-2010, my son and I moved out of the apartment and moved in with one of my older sisters home. My son Aron was 10 years old I had full custody of my son living in with my sister and her children. I was going through a brokeness phase of life. God sees and knows how my son and I felt. God had spoken to me and told me "Read Genesis chapters 1, 2, and 3 and teach it to your son. Out of obedience, I did so, we fasted, prayed, and read the Word together. At this point, my son and I were broken in our hearts but I believed that the Lord was preparing us for something. Although I hadn't figured it out yet I believed God was telling us to read these chapters. At this time Aron was in the 4th grade going to Martin Luther King Elementary School and my son never gave up and we stuck together. I kept him focused on GOD, on school, and playing football.

My son, Aron had won so many trophies playing for a few teams, winning tournament championships in the Peewee (8 and 9) and Junior (10 and 11) division. A few months went by getting closer to the summer break for school I got my son, Aron, and his Cousins (my nephew and nieces) and took them over to their other cousin's house where we were there for a few hours.

While there I received a phone call from my mother saying that my sister's house was on fire. I was in disbelief, we got the kids back in the car and raced back to the house. As we approached and got closer we could see large flames in the air. The reality hit us that the house was on fire, all the things that we had brought with us from moving were lost in the fire; my belongings, my son's championship trophies, some of my father's pictures. We were facing not having a place to live. I called Brother Jacque and told him what had happened, he told me he would call me back.

Moments later I received a call back from Brother Jacque and he told us to come and stay at his grandfather's house until we got our things together. We stayed at his grandfather's house and were so thankful no one had lost their lives in the fire just materialistic things.

God began to use Deacon Morris to bless us while staying with them temporarily. Having food and shelter was a blessing and it taught me and my son. We were also blessed with the help of people connecting from my job at that time and receiving donations from the South Eastern Christian Church. Eventually, we moved into our new apartment, "To God be the Glory."

However, I received my divorce papers in the mail, and I told my son it was over, he was sad but at the same time he encouraged me by saying, "Daddy it's going to be all right, God is going to send you somebody else." About two months after the divorce was final, I got fired from my job, no income coming in and I was looking for a new job. My Son had no idea what was going on.

There is now an eviction notice on our door and we have nowhere to go, at this time. I got so angry I just gave up on God and went back into my worldly ways.

My son witnessed my change of events at this point in my life. His Godfather, my best friend, said it was ok for us to live with them temporarily.

Moving from place to place was exhausting living with family and their rules and regulations was better than not having a place to live. I have started back drinking Budweiser, going to clubs, and making money by working temp jobs being a full-time dad was no excuse for this behavior, I just chose to do it being selfish. My son was watching my behavior and watching me change from good to bad living with my family temporarily for four months. I am still taking my son to school and football practice, and supporting the nominee's games helped take my mind off what was going on.

I received information on how to get some money for us which seemed so easy to do, but I was not thinking about my son. I was being tempted and imagining us with a way out, thinking how my son and I could live with this money. So this particular night the kids were asleep, and the plan was set right before us.

At 12:00 midnight was the time to go and make our move and get ($15,000) a piece. Right before we were ready to go and make that move, the Lord spoke to me and said, "If you go through with this.....this will be your last day on Earth!"

Suddenly a fear hit me that I cannot describe till this day and I did not go through with the plans. Of course, they got mad at me and had some words with me concerning that situation. They went on to pursue the plan, I stayed home and fell asleep.

The next morning I asked them "So did y'all get it."

They said “no” because there were children there so we turned it down. I began to think and put two-two together, God was saving those children for what was about to happen and if anything was going to happen with that family, God was going to let my life be taken that day.

Immediately afterward, with conviction in my heart, I decided then to give my life back to the Lord and I did with no hesitation.

My family didn't understand it, but I did so out of obedience, my son and I gave our lives back to the Lord in January of 2010. My son, my nephew, and I became members of Bible Way C.O.G.I.C.

DID YOU KNOW?

Gun violence is a significant concern in Memphis, Tennessee, as it is in many urban areas across the United States. The issue is multifaceted, involving social, economic, and systemic factors. Here's an overview of the situation and contributing elements:

Current Trends

1. Crime Rates: Memphis consistently ranks among the cities with higher crime rates in the U.S. Gun-related crimes, including homicides, assaults, and robberies, contribute significantly to these statistics.
2. Youth Involvement: A substantial portion of gun violence involves young people, either as perpetrators or victims, often linked to gang activity or disputes.
3. Domestic Violence: Many instances of gun violence in Memphis are related to domestic disputes.
4. Community Impact: Gun violence disproportionately affects certain neighborhoods, particularly those facing high poverty rates and limited access to education or resources.

Contributing Factors

1. Poverty: Memphis has a higher-than-average poverty rate, which can lead to desperation and crime as a means of survival.
2. Gun Accessibility: Tennessee has relatively lenient gun laws, which may contribute to the prevalence of firearms in the community.
3. Lack of Resources: Many affected neighborhoods lack adequate community programs, mental health resources, and opportunities for youth engagement.
4. Systemic Challenges: Underfunded schools, limited employment opportunities, and historical systemic inequalities exacerbate the problem.

Efforts to Address Gun Violence

1. Community Initiatives: Local organizations are working to provide resources, mentorship, and alternatives for at-risk youth.
2. Law Enforcement: Memphis Police Department has implemented various strategies, such as community policing and task forces, to reduce violent crime.
3. Legislative Measures: There are ongoing debates about gun control policies, though significant changes at the state level remain contentious.
4. Nonprofits and Advocacy Groups: Organizations like Moms Demand Action and community-led efforts are raising awareness and pushing for policy changes.

What Can Be Done?

1. Strengthen Community Programs: More investment in education,

after-school programs, and vocational training can provide alternatives to violence.

1. Policy Reform: Advocating for balanced gun laws that respect rights while prioritizing safety could mitigate access to firearms for those likely to commit crimes.
2. Increased Funding: Public funding for community centers, mental health services, and housing assistance can address root causes.
3. Engage Local Leadership: Working with local leaders to address systemic inequities and build trust between communities and law enforcement.

If you'd like specific data or updates on current initiatives in Memphis, I can look into that for you. Let me know!

CHAPTER 5

A SECOND CHANCE

JAMES 4:10 "Humble yourself [with an attitude of repentance and insignificance] in the presence of the Lord, and He will exalt you [He will lift you, He will give you purpose].

"Christians should repent and move close to God again. We should trust Him to provide, to be the Judge, and to lift us up in His time. In humility, we must acknowledge that all of our plans are dependent on Him, and He can change them at any moment."

Now it's 2010 living in our new apartment this time as a single father raising up an 11-year-old 5th grader transferring schools from Martin Luther King Elementary to Trunnell Elementary School where he had graduated from, it was pretty busy. In church, we joined the band. My son learned how to play the trumpet, my nephew learned how to play the trombone and I was playing the saxophone. We would go to other church functions and play songs.

Also, my son was playing football for the Shawnee Eagle (Junior Division) one thing for sure I kept my son busy trying to keep him out of the streets while living in Louisville Kentucky. Living for God now with good guidance kept me at peace. So while this was going on I found a new job where I worked the second shift 5 pm - 1 am as a floor technician.

For a few months, things were going well for us, until the rent lady sold the apartment complex where eventually we had to move. I now have a new job without a place to stay so me and my son didn't let that bother us we believe God that he will make a way. It's May, my son is graduating from 5th grade from Elementary to Middle School. Now it's summertime and we are still living in the apartment where God gave us His favor and more time at the apartment.

One particular night at work while doing the floors at Walgreens in Louisville Kentucky that was off Shelbyville Road, the manager and employee began to ask me questions about God. God began to use me to tell them about the goodness of God. While this conversation was going on my coworker was watching and listening. When we finished the store and I got into the work van my friend (co-worker) turned around and looked at me and said, "You are a preacher, you are a man of God I know a preacher when I hear one and I'm much older than you and I've been around for a while to know this, I was raised in church." I replied and said, "Please!"

He responded and said, "Do you know how long you were talking to them?"

I replied "No."

He said, "You were preaching to them for a whole hour; you are a preacher!"

So now with that on my mind and trying to figure out where my son and I are going to live. This particular Sunday my pastor at that time, I was always in the back working with the sound system for the church at the end of my pastor's message said, "The Lord said that there is someone here that has been running from their calling to God; stop running!"

When I heard that it quickly thought of what God had encouraged my coworker to tell me that I was a preacher. I was nervous and scared but the Lord said, "Go."

I began to walk up front to the altar. I looked at my pastor and told him it was me, I accepted my calling as a preacher.

My son stood up and everybody in the church stood up and started applauding. That Sunday, December 26, 2010, at 7:00 pm, it was official.

Looking at my son and being touched by God, I was encouraged to write a reconciliation letter to my ex-wife, wanting a second chance to be a family again. I got the letter blessed and the letter was mailed. There was no response, so the Lord said, "Stay focused, everything's going to be all right." Now a couple of months have gone by and still no response. So we eventually moved and put a lot of our belongings in storage in November and moved in with one of my older sisters on the east side of Louisville Kentucky.

DID YOU KNOW?

Gun violence in Atlanta, Georgia, is a pressing issue, reflecting broader national trends while also having unique local factors. Atlanta's position as a major metropolitan area contributes to the complexity of addressing this problem. Here's an overview of gun violence in Atlanta:

Current Trends

1. Homicides: Gun-related homicides have been a significant portion of violent crime in Atlanta, with spikes in recent years mirroring national trends.
2. Youth Involvement: As in other cities, a notable percentage of gun violence involves young people, often linked to gang activity or interpersonal disputes.
3. Neighborhood Disparities: Gun violence is concentrated in certain neighborhoods, many of which face systemic poverty, unemployment, and lack of resources.
4. Car Break-ins: Atlanta has seen an increase in firearms stolen from vehicles, contributing to the illegal circulation of guns.

Contributing Factors

1. Access to Firearms: Georgia has relatively permissive gun laws, including constitutional carry, which allows carrying a handgun without a permit. This accessibility can increase the likelihood of guns being used in crimes.
2. Economic Inequality: Wealth disparities in Atlanta contribute to crime rates, as poverty and lack of opportunity are key drivers of violence.
3. Gang Activity: Organized and street-level gang activity contributes to gun violence in specific areas.
4. Domestic Violence: Many instances of gun violence in Atlanta are tied to domestic situations, highlighting the need for intervention in family and relational conflicts.

Efforts to Address Gun Violence

1. Community-Based Programs: Organizations like Cure Violence and other local nonprofits work on violence prevention by engaging at-risk youth and mediating conflicts.
2. Police Strategies: The Atlanta Police Department has implemented initiatives like increasing officer presence in high-crime areas and using technology such as ShotSpotter to detect gunfire.
3. Legislative Advocacy: Groups like Moms Demand Action and Everytown for Gun Safety advocate for stricter gun laws and policies at the state and federal levels.
4. Youth Engagement: Programs aimed at providing job training, mentorship, and extracurricular opportunities are being expanded in some communities.

Challenges

1. Limited Resources: Some neighborhoods lack sufficient funding for schools, community centers, and public services that could prevent violence.
2. Public Trust: Building trust between law enforcement and communities has been a challenge, particularly in neighborhoods that feel over-policed yet underserved.
3. State vs. Local Control: Georgia's state laws often limit the ability of cities like Atlanta to implement stricter local gun control measures.

What Can Be Done?

1. Stronger Gun Laws: Advocating for measures such as universal background checks, safe storage laws, and restrictions on gun ownership for individuals with a history of violence.
2. Investment in Communities: Expanding funding for education, affordable housing, and mental health resources.
3. Conflict Mediation: Supporting programs that intervene in disputes before they escalate to violence.
4. Engaging Youth: Offering alternative pathways through mentorship, education, and employment opportunities.

Would you like details about specific programs or data in Atlanta, or resources for involvement? Let me know!

CHAPTER 6
THE TESTING TIMES

Be assured that the testing of your faith [through experience] produces endurance [leading to spiritual maturity, and inner peace]. And let endurance have its perfect result and do a thorough work, so that you may be perfect and completely developed [in your faith], lacking in nothing.
James 1:3-4

"Just as a rose, you cannot gather that fragrant flower without the presence of its rough companion, the thorn. Therefore, you cannot have faith without experiencing the trials of life, because faith and trials go together. He wants us to be mature."

Now after, accepting my calling to the ministry, in 2011, Aron was 12 years old in the 6th grade and making good grades at this time living with my other oldest sister Tracy.

In the 7th grade, at Mazeek Middle School in Louisville, Kentucky, Aron was making good grades at this living with my other oldest Sister Tracy who lived on the East side of the City.

I received a phone call from my ex-wife telling me that she enjoyed my "Trial Sermon" message on Sunday night, December 26, 2010. She said that message convicted her on some things. So I smiled and said, "To God be the Glory, and thank you". We began to talk again and it led to dating again and Aron was so happy.

Living with my sister was putting her in bad situations because she was in a living program; where no one was allowed to live with her so we were sneaking to live there. It starting to cause conflict with us living there. I began to get telephone calls from Aron's School telling me, he was itching and scratching himself in the classroom. At that time, I didn't understand what was going on, but it was "Bed Bugs" that was biting him while he was asleep. We began exterminating the whole house killing all the "Bed Bugs." We did get rid of the "Bed Bugs."

One night I was about to sleep, and an argument started between my sister and her friend. At that time I was trying to be a peacemaker, being tested and tried with both and threats from a friend, I had to turn the other cheek. This went on for a couple of months until my sister had to force us to move because of the drama. So again nowhere to go we were forced to move in with my mother. So at this time, my ex-wife and I were looking for a place to move in together; having my hopes up thinking that we were going to renew our vows (get married again) so we were getting our things together to move in my mother's house. Aron and I finally moved into my mother's house living on the Northwest side of Louisville, Kentucky.

In the Portland Neighborhood on St. Xavier Street, the house was crowded with my son, myself, and three of my brothers making it the best we can with the help of the Lord. I was dating my ex-wife for a couple of months within that year. One particular day I received a phone call from my ex-wife (at this time Aron was in school) saying we can't continue like this for me to marry you again. You have two priorities before we do anything.

First, you have to get a better-paying job and secondly, get us a place to live and, maybe then I might consider moving in and marrying you again. Until then I don't wanna be with you. So my heart was broken again, and God began to minister to me concerning her.

I told her what the Lord told me to tell her, "If you close this door that God had opened back up for reconciliation of marriage, He said that door that you close for us will not open back up again". Her response was "Oh well, God is still going to bless me without you". God told me, "Do not beg her back let her move on with that decision". I replied "YES LORD" and from that day on we went on separate ways. I told my son when he got out of school, he looked at me and said again "God has someone else for you, don't sweat it, Daddy". Now, we are at my mother's house in the summer of 2011 as we continue to stay faithful to God while we are in our test.

DID YOU KNOW?

Gun violence is a significant and persistent issue in Baltimore, Maryland, deeply rooted in systemic and socioeconomic challenges. Here's an overview of the situation:

Current Trends

1. High Homicide Rates: Baltimore consistently ranks among U.S. cities with the highest homicide rates per capita. Most homicides involve firearms.
2. Concentrated Violence: Gun violence is heavily concentrated in specific neighborhoods, often those struggling with poverty, unemployment, and disinvestment.
3. Youth Victims and Perpetrators: Many gun violence incidents involve young people, whether as victims or participants, often linked to gang-related activities or personal disputes.
4. Retaliatory Violence: A significant portion of gun violence in Baltimore stems from cycles of retaliation between individuals or groups.

Contributing Factors

1. Poverty and Inequality: Baltimore has a high poverty rate, and the disparities in wealth and opportunity contribute to crime and violence.
2. Drug Trade: The illegal drug economy has historically fueled violence in Baltimore, as disputes over territories and sales escalate to gunfire.
3. Access to Firearms: Maryland has stricter gun laws compared to some states, but illegal firearms trafficking still leads to widespread availability of guns.
4. Underfunded Services: Many neighborhoods lack adequate resources, including quality education, mental health services, and job training programs.

Impact on Communities

- Economic Consequences: Gun violence discourages investment and economic growth in affected neighborhoods.
- Trauma: Residents, especially children, often experience PTSD and other mental health challenges due to exposure to violence.
- Community Distrust: There is a deep-seated mistrust between residents and law enforcement, complicating efforts to address the problem collaboratively.

Efforts to Address Gun Violence

1. Community Violence Interruption:
    - Programs like Safe Streets employ individuals with credibility in their neighborhoods to mediate conflicts and prevent retaliatory violence.

2. Law Enforcement Strategies:
   - Baltimore Police Department has implemented data-driven strategies to focus on high-risk areas and individuals.
   - Collaboration with federal agencies to target illegal firearms trafficking.
3. Legislative Efforts:
   - Maryland has enacted gun control measures like requiring background checks and banning certain high-capacity weapons.
   - Efforts to close loopholes and address ghost guns are ongoing.
4. Grassroots Movements:
   - Organizations and activists are pushing for holistic solutions that address root causes like poverty and lack of education.
5. Youth Programs:
   - Initiatives such as mentoring, after-school activities, and workforce development aim to provide alternatives to violence.

Challenges

1. Lack of Trust in Law Enforcement: Historical instances of corruption and misconduct have strained police-community relations.
2. Systemic Issues: Generational poverty, racial segregation, and underinvestment in infrastructure remain significant barriers.
3. Limited Resources: Programs like Safe Streets are often underfunded and limited in scale.

Cycle of Violence: Breaking the cycle of retaliation requires sustained, multi-faceted approaches that address both immediate and long-term needs.

Possible Solutions

1. Expanding Community Programs: Scaling up successful programs like Safe Streets and increasing funding for community-based initiatives.
2. Addressing Root Causes: Investing in education, healthcare, affordable housing, and employment opportunities.
3. Strengthening Gun Laws: Continued advocacy for measures to reduce the flow of illegal firearms into Baltimore.
4. Building Trust: Efforts to improve police accountability and community engagement.
5. Trauma Support: Expanding access to mental health resources for individuals and families affected by violence.

CHAPTER 7

PRE-TEEN BEGINNINGS

Fathers, do not provoke your children to anger [do not exasperate them to the point of resentment with demands that are trivial or unreasonable or humiliating or abusive; nor by showing favoritism or indifference to any of them], but bring them up [tenderly, with lovingkindness] in the discipline and instruction of the Lord.
Ephesians 6:4

Ephesians 6:4 connects not provoking children to anger with bringing them up as God has instructed. God calls all parents to treat their children with love in all situations. That's how God relates to us as his spiritual children. So, this verse points to God's example of what parenting should look like.

It's still the year 2011, Aron at the age of 12 (a pre-teen transferring from Meyzeek Middle School to Westport Middle School,) was a young football star, running back in the senior division for the Shawnee Eagles. He also was playing AAU Basketball. Although Aron was on his way to becoming a teenager he was a proper kid in school. I was busy coming and going, having to take him to football games over there and basketball games over here. At times as a father with a very energetic Son was pretty exhausting to me, at times he would tell me, "Daddy you know I have a Game today" or "Daddy you know I have a Basketball game tomorrow."

My response was ok let's go. At this point in his life, He was beginning to smell himself a little bit. I wasn't used to or wasn't trying to understand what was happening but at times I was frustrated. I'm trying to get things together for us but at the same time living with my mother, and helping her with the bills didn't make things much easier.

As a minister in the family now, I was trying to be a peacemaker. There were times when my brothers would argue back and forth with each other to the point where they wanted to fight each other. Nephews were in and out of the house, causing distraction.

While I was trying to be a peacemaker my son would sneak out somewhere to hang out with his friends, but I had to discipline him at times when he tried to explain to me why. I didn't listen to him, being a single father and a really strict parent. With anger and frustration living in a house of six with us all being males, brothers, and nephews was tough. Everybody was clashing with disagreements and arguments, nearly breaking out into fights. My son witnessed all these events and it made him resentful at times to me. Being so caught up in distractions I was not seeing the red flags of my son's behaviors in school and out of school. Come to find out my son had a girlfriend he had met through his cousin this is what I found out later on.

"FATHER : SON"
FATHER'S DAY
2011

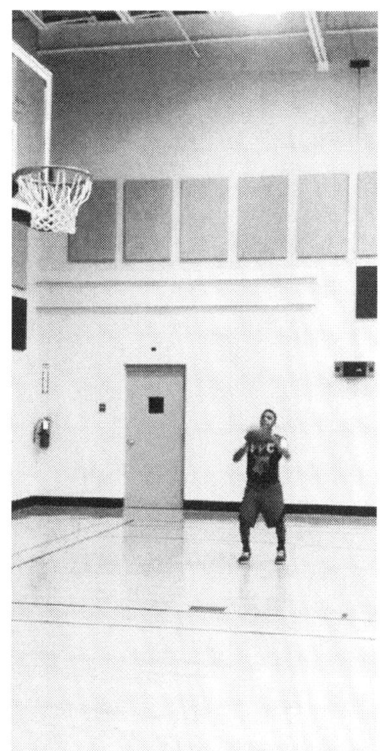

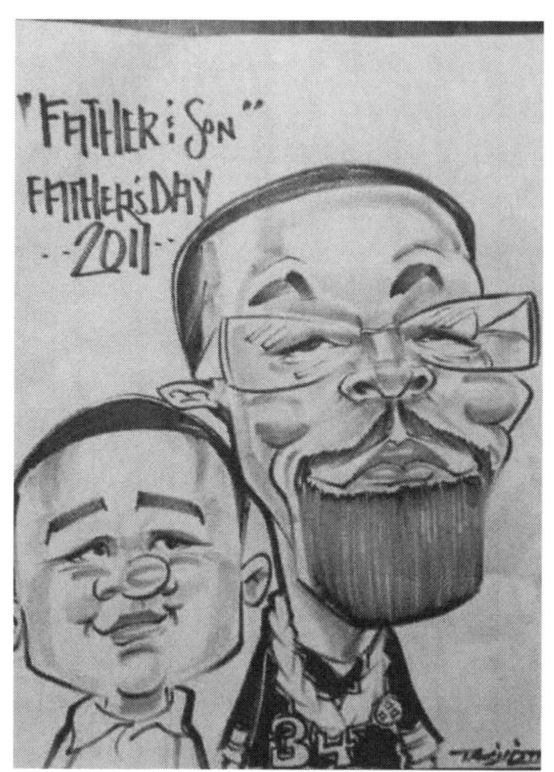

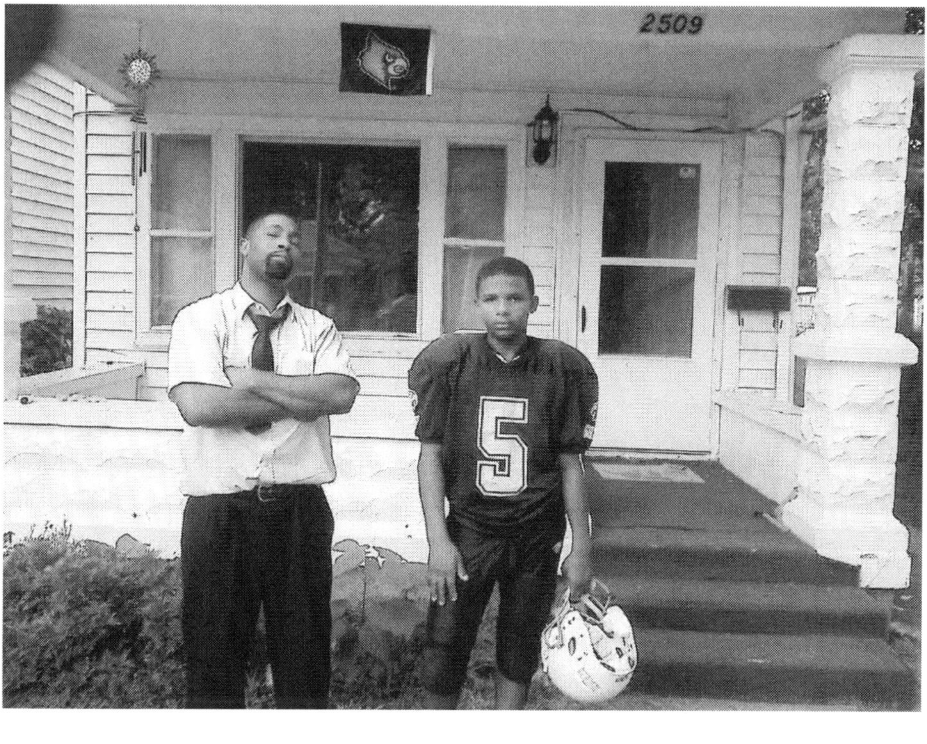
2509

DID YOU KNOW?

Gun violence in Detroit, Michigan, is a critical issue with deep ties to systemic challenges, socioeconomic conditions, and historical factors. Here's a comprehensive overview:

Current Trends

1. Homicides and Shootings: Detroit has consistently high rates of gun-related homicides and non-fatal shootings compared to other U.S. cities. Firearms are involved in the majority of violent crimes.
2. Youth and Gun Violence: Many incidents involve young people as both victims and perpetrators, often linked to gang activity or interpersonal disputes.
3. Neighborhood Impact: Gun violence is concentrated in specific neighborhoods that experience higher levels of poverty, unemployment, and disinvestment.
4. Community Trauma: Persistent gun violence creates an environment of fear and psychological stress for residents, particularly children.

Contributing Factors

1. Economic Challenges: Detroit has one of the highest poverty rates among large U.S. cities, with limited access to economic opportunities fueling criminal activity.
2. Gun Accessibility: Michigan's gun laws are moderately regulated, but illegal firearm trafficking contributes to the availability of guns in the city.
3. Gang Activity and Drug Trade: Territorial disputes and conflicts over the illegal drug trade are major drivers of gun violence in Detroit.
4. Systemic Inequities: Generations of racial segregation, underfunded schools, and limited access to resources exacerbate conditions that lead to violence.

Impact on Communities

- Economic Effects: Gun violence discourages investment, increases costs for law enforcement and healthcare, and limits the economic growth of affected neighborhoods.
- Psychological Effects: Chronic exposure to gun violence contributes to high rates of PTSD, depression, and anxiety, particularly among children.
- Family Disruption: Families often face long-term emotional and financial strain due to the loss of loved ones or injury.

Efforts to Address Gun Violence

- Community Policing and Partnerships:
    - Detroit Police Department (DPD) collaborates with community organizations to build trust and address violence proactively

- Programs like Ceasefire Detroit aim to interrupt cycles of retaliation through outreach and intervention.

1. Violence Interruption:
   - Organizations like Detroit Life is Valuable Everyday (DLIVE) focus on hospital-based interventions to prevent repeat shootings.
2. Legislative Measures:
   - Efforts to strengthen background checks, regulate ghost guns, and address straw purchases are ongoing in Michigan.
3. Youth Engagement:
   - Programs such as Grow Detroit's Young Talent and mentorship initiatives aim to provide alternatives for at-risk youth.
4. Community Investment:
   - Initiatives like Detroit Future City work to address root causes of violence by improving education, creating jobs, and revitalizing neighborhoods.

Challenges

1. Trust in Law Enforcement: Historical tensions between residents and police make collaboration challenging, particularly in underserved neighborhoods.
2. Poverty and Disinvestment: Addressing gun violence requires substantial investment in addressing long-standing economic and social disparities.
3. Illegal Firearms: Despite regulatory measures, the flow of illegal firearms into Detroit remains a significant issue.

- Resource Limitations: Programs targeting gun violence often face funding shortages, limiting their reach and effectiveness.

Possible Solutions

1. Expanding Community Programs: Increase funding and support for grassroots organizations and violence interruption programs.
2. Economic Development: Invest in job training, education, and affordable housing to address the root causes of gun violence.
3. Gun Control Measures: Advocate for stronger background checks, mandatory safe storage laws, and efforts to combat illegal gun trafficking.
4. Trauma-Informed Care: Enhance access to mental health resources and trauma support for individuals and families affected by violence.
5. Data-Driven Strategies: Use technology and analytics to identify high-risk areas and individuals for targeted interventions.

Detroit's response to gun violence requires a holistic approach that addresses immediate safety concerns while tackling the underlying causes. If you'd like detailed information about programs, policies, or ways to get involved in Detroit's anti-violence efforts, let me know!

CHAPTER 8
THE YEAR OF CHAMPIONS

Yet in all these things we are more than conquerors and gain an overwhelming victory through Him who loved us [so much that He died for us].
Romans 8:37

To be more than a conqueror means that before you ever get a problem, you already know that whatever problem comes your way, you can overcome it through Christ. You live with confidence that God loves you no matter what and He will never leave you nor forsake you.

Now it's 2012 and Aron was 13 years old, at 5'6 in his second year senior season of the Youth Football Division for the Shawnee Eagles Youth football team. It was a hard-working season in his life, preparation for the game consistency, and being on time for practice. I was at this time a Parent Coach helping the coaches coach the kids. I was an active parent and a participant on the coaching staff with the Head Coach Sean. He was a big-time San Francisco 49ers and my son was one of his favorite players on the team. Meanwhile, back at home, it was an exciting year for our city Louisville, Kentucky at the University of Louisville in the football sports program. At this time the University of Louisville Football Head Coach, Charlie Strong, had youth football Camps around the city. My son's head coach had his senior players register into Coach Charlie Strong Youth Football Camps.

Coach Strong would watch my son's skills on the field and would say to Coach Sean, "That Boy is Good! Whose son is that?" Coach Sean would reply with a laugh or giggle. I would feel so good when I got reports that the Coach of the League wanted my Son to play for them. I just smiled from ear to ear and said to myself, "That's my boy." The Shawnee Eagles ended up winning the best of the best championship that year. At this time, the University of Louisville basketball team was in the Big East Conference The same year (2012) The Louisville Cardinals basketball program ended their season in the final four tournament against a really good opponent the Kentucky Wildcats Who had won it that year the national championship. Aron was in the 8th Grade going to Westport Middle where had later graduated. The year 2012 was exciting in Sports. I was coaching my son at home, preparing him for football and basketball games. I just knew that my son was going to be something in life and become the first in our own immediate family, an NFL star one day, I was so very PROUD of him.

23
36
57

36
23
5

34
23

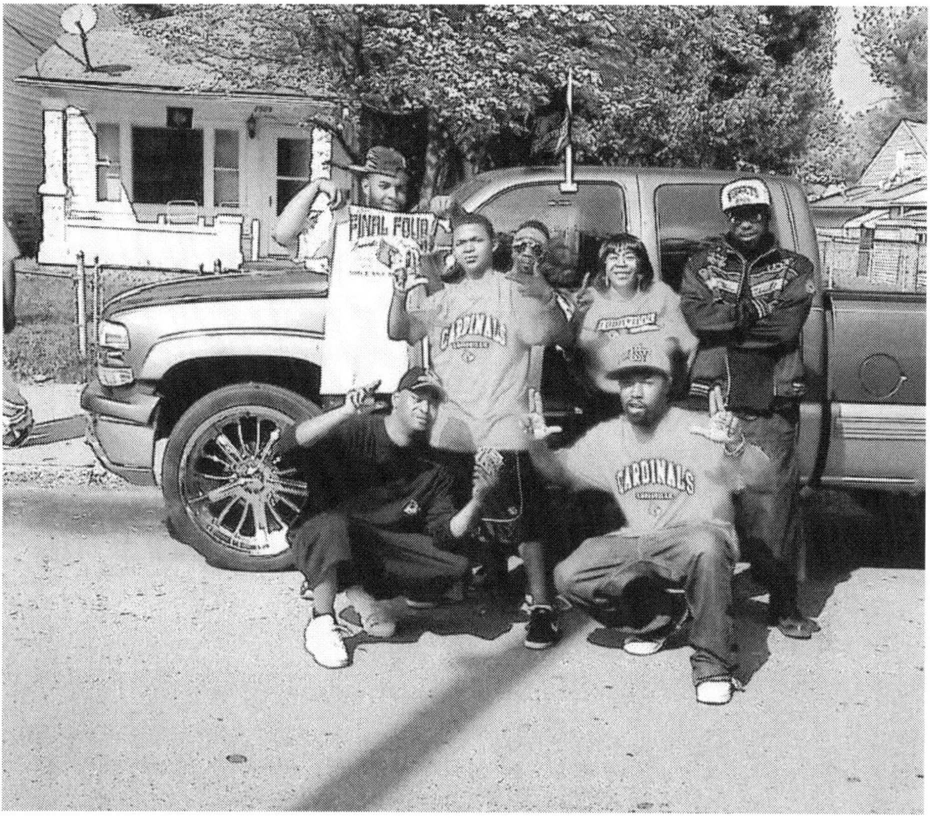
FINAL FOUR
CARDINALS
CARDINALS

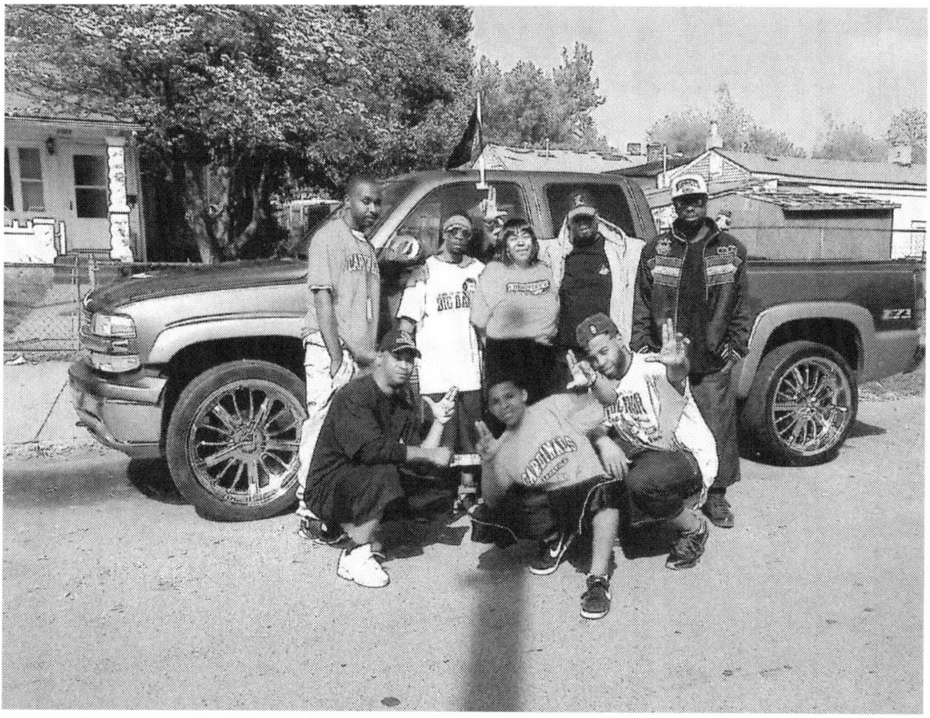
CARDINALS

DID YOU KNOW?

Gun violence remains a significant concern in Chicago, Illinois, though recent data indicates a downward trend in such incidents. Here's an overview of the current statistics and trends:

Recent Statistics

- Homicides and Shootings: As of September 2024, Chicago recorded 439 homicides and 1,808 shootings, marking decreases of 8% and 5%, respectively, compared to the same period in 2023.
- Summer Trends: The summer of 2024 experienced the smallest surge in gun violence rates in six years, indicating progress in violence reduction efforts.
- Center for American Progress
    - https://www.americanprogress.org/article/2024-sees-smallest-summer-surge-in-gun-violence-rates-in-6-years/?utm_source=chatgpt.com
- Mass Shootings: In 2024, Chicago has experienced multiple mass shootings, contributing to the overall gun violence statistics.
- Wikipedia: https://en.wikipedia.org/wiki/List_of_mass_shootings_in_the_United_States_in_2024?utm_source=chatgpt.com

- Comparative Analysis
- Year-over-Year Comparison: The reductions in homicides and shootings in 2024 continue a positive trend from previous years, suggesting that intervention strategies may be yielding results.
- National Context: Despite these improvements, Chicago has been labeled America's "murder capital" for the 12th consecutive year, with 617 homicides in 2023, reflecting a 50% increase from 2013.
- New York Post
    - https://nypost.com/2024/08/19/us-news/chicago-earns-disturbing-title-of-americas-murder-capital-as-dnc-kicks-off/?utm_source=chatgpt.com
- Contributing Factors
- Community Initiatives: Programs focusing on violence interruption and community engagement are believed to play a role in the recent declines in gun violence.
- Law Enforcement Strategies: Enhanced policing efforts, including data-driven approaches and increased patrols in high-crime areas, have been implemented to address gun violence.
- Ongoing Challenges
- Persistent Violence: Despite the downward trends, gun violence remains a critical issue, with certain neighborhoods disproportionately affected.
- Resource Allocation: Sustaining and expanding successful intervention programs require continuous funding and community support.

Conclusion

- While Chicago has made notable progress in reducing gun violence in 2024, ongoing efforts are essential to address the underlying causes and sustain these improvements.

CHAPTER 9
JUMPING OF THE TORCH

"Brother will betray brother to death, and the father his child; and children will rise up and rebel against their parents and cause them to be put to death."
Matthew 10:21

"When people realize it is the living God you are representing and not some idol that makes them feel good, they will turn on you, even people in your own family."

Now it is the year 2013 and we are living at 3439 Larkwood Ave. My son is now turning 14 years old at 5'9. This was a GREAT year in the city of Louisville, Kentucky, the Cardinals Men's Basketball team won the National Championship. I am super excited about everyone's accomplishment, my son graduated from the eighth grade to the ninth grade. He and his cousin are going to the same middle school. Graduating at the same time I thought was pretty cool. I am still working at FMS as a Floor Technician & working in the church. Aron was meeting new friends at our new address and being the new kid on the block (Neighborhood). There was so much going on that year in 2013, our church was busy traveling up-and-down 65 North South Bend, Gary, Fort Wayne, and Indianapolis, IN. In the same year, I was ordained as an Elder in the C.O.G.I.C. under the leadership of Supt. John C. Robinson Sr in the 4th Ecclesiastical North Indiana Jurisdiction under Bishop Donald L. Alford Sr., Prelate.

While everything was going on some things were causing a big distraction. I wasn't 100% focused on my son and his well-being. It was things he was getting into; it was the little foxes that destroyed the Vine, but it was very hard to notice things. At this time being a single parent raising a 14-year-old teen, his mother was in and out of his life which was causing an imbalance in his life. He was being pulled in all directions.

Living with my mother with my three brothers was not helping as I found that out later on. Now it's spring going into summer, I'm working hard on the 3rd shift. My co-worker and I were scheduled to do this doctor's office but this particular doctor's office had to have security watch us. When we were getting set up to do this floor we needed more supplies and my co-worker volunteered to go and get the supplies. While I was waiting for him this security guard was reading a book. I asked him what is it that you are reading? He replied, "Oh reading about this man of God," he did not know that I was a man of God as well, so I replied, "That's interesting so what church do you go to?" That opened up the door for a long conversation as we went back and forth touching and agreeing and talking about God. I will never forget what happened. Next, the presence of the Lord came into that office and the security guard began to speak in tongues as the spirit of the Lord gave him utterance.

After he spoke in tongues the Lord gave him the Interpretation and he began to prophesy about my life and everything that was prophesied to me back in March 10, 2002. The tears began to fall down my face. God told him to call one of the Mothers who go to his church to confirm what was said to me. She answered the phone and when she heard the sound of my voice she began to prophesy everything he had told me to confirm God's word.

Afterward, he said to me "The Lord said for you to get away from the women you are associated with because the levels God is about to put you on are above them, they will tear you down also the Lord said that your Wife will not be of this State or this City the Lord said it won't be many days hence from now". And while he was ministering to me my hands went up and I said, "YES LORD! YES LORD! YES LORD!" So about two months after the prophecy here come my Wife but at the time I did not know who she was and my son didn't either and the prophecy was true she was not of this atate or city so about a month after she came to our church and became a Member of Bible Way C.O.G.I.C. The Lord spoke into my ear and told me during service "That is your Wife".

After hearing that it took a while for me to grasp hold until God one day revealed my prayer to me what I prayed about two years ago. I asked for a wife, and my son needed a mother involved in his life. I then pursued after her as my son watched this unfold before him; he was very happy for me. But shortly after my son's behavior began to change. Getting into fights in High School, he was not coming home like he should, getting phone calls from the school, kicked off the Football Team, and doing sneaky things running in the streets. Public School eventually kicked him out and sent him to Buechel High School.

Before I got married on December 26, 2013, he had told me that when I would be on my way to work he did not come home because of the mistreatment he was getting with some of his cousins and uncles that he wanted to live with his mother. So at this stage of life, he was very resentful towards the family so it was making him rebellious. I tried to convince him not to go and told him it was going to get better for us because God was making a way for us but he did not want to listen and receive. So I continue to pray and stay focused on December 26, 2013, my wedding date.

WAGGENER
25

NCAA
2013

CARDINALS

FOOTBALL
VILLE

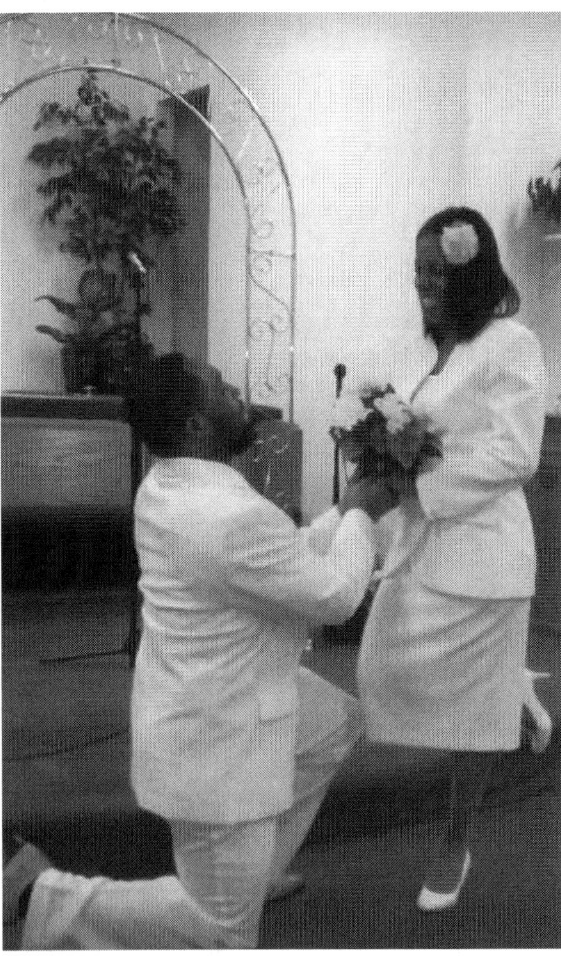

DID YOU KNOW?

Gun violence in Tampa, Florida, has been a growing concern in recent years, with notable increases in firearm-related incidents. Here's an overview of the current statistics and trends:

Recent Statistics

- Homicides Involving Firearms: Tampa has experienced a rise in deadly shootings over the past few years. The number of firearm-related homicides increased from 19 in 2019 to 38 in 2022.
- Violent Crime Involving Firearms: In 2022, Tampa reported a nearly 6% decrease in violent crimes involving firearms compared to the previous year. However, the city has seen a gradual rise in deadly shootings since the pandemic began.
- Recent Incidents: As of June 2024, there has been a noticeable increase in fatal shootings, including incidents in neighborhoods like Hyde Park and New Tampa, where such crimes are typically rare.

Comparative Analysis

- National Trends: While violent crime has been decreasing nationally, Tampa's recent uptick in gun violence contrasts with these broader trends.
- Local Comparisons: Neighboring cities, such as St. Petersburg,

have reported decreases in violent crime, highlighting the unique challenges Tampa faces in addressing gun violence.

Contributing Factors

- Pandemic Impact: Local law enforcement attributes the rise in gun violence to the onset of the COVID-19 pandemic, which has exacerbated economic and social stressors.
- Stolen Firearms: A significant number of guns used in crimes are stolen from unlocked vehicles, contributing to the proliferation of illegal firearms on the streets.

Efforts to Address Gun Violence

- Law Enforcement Strategies: The Tampa Police Department has emphasized community collaboration and proactive policing to combat the rise in gun violence. Interim Chief Lee Bercaw highlighted the importance of community involvement in crime reduction efforts.
- Community Initiatives: Survivors and advocacy groups are raising awareness and seeking solutions to address the root causes of gun violence in the city.

Conclusion

Despite a reported decrease in overall violent crime involving firearms in recent years, Tampa continues to face challenges with rising deadly shootings. Ongoing efforts by law enforcement and community organizations aim to reverse this trend and enhance public safety. For more detailed and up-to-date information, the Tampa Police Department provides an Interactive Crime Map that offers geocoded data on specific crimes within the city.

CHAPTER 10
"REBELLIOUS TIME"

"Woe (judgment is coming) to the rebellious children," declares the Lord, "Who carry out a plan, but not Mine, And make an alliance [by pouring out a libation], but not of My Spirit, In order to add sin to sin;
Isaiah 30:1

"If someone is rebellious, they are difficult to control and do not behave in the way that is expected."

It's the year of 2014 Aron is 15 years old. As a newlywed to my gorgeous wife, Valerie J Ware, we are living off Preston Hwy and this was new for him. Without a mother figure and being just my son and me from 2009-2013, it was hard for him to get used to now having a mother figure in the home. At this time in his life, he was dibbling and dabbling in the streets. Before my wife and I got married there were two incidents my son was involved in. The first incident was on the school bus where his friend was getting bullied and my son stepped in and beat that guy up. The second incident happened when three guys tried to jump him (fight him at once) in high school. The word was that my Son had beaten them up. They didn't know when my son was about 5 years old, I taught him how to box and defend himself. So instead of one week of suspension, they kicked him out of "Waggner High School, he was suspended from school indefinitely. My son got into some street altercations which led him in and out of Juvenile Corrections and in and out of the courthouses.

Around this time, he was sent to "Buechel Minor" called "Minor Daniels Academy". He was sent there because of his indefinite suspension for two years. After which he was eligible to go back to public school. He was so upset that he stopped caring about school at this point. My son began cutting school and getting in trouble in the streets. At this point, as his father, I was getting so frustrated because the court system was threatening to lock me up for truancy (the action of staying away from school without good reason).

The judge decided to put him on house arrest (ankle watch). It worked for a while but I guess our home rules were too much for him. Our home rules were submitted under GOD authority, the Word of God. My son became rebellious, while we were at work he would bring his best friend over and they were in his room smoking weed. One day Momma V came home and found weed in his room, she told me and I confronted him about it. Of course, he denied that it was his and tried to blame Momma V. At that point, I became very angry and grabbed him and shoved him to the wall. I told his best friend to LEAVE!! Momma V being Mom, talked to me and I realized I was being a little bit too harsh even though our son tried to blame her. In spite of my son blaming Mommy V, she still showed him more LOVE to the point my son's eyes were filled with tears, he was crying.

I calmed down and apologized for my action. We begin to minister to our son. One day when we got home from work, I went into his room, looked and realized he had cut off his ankle watch, jumped out the window, and ran away from home. Months has gone by and he had not come home yet. One particular day I received a phone call from a Juvenile Correctional Facility, he had been arrested. He was going back and forth to Court where they kept him for a few months in the Juvenile Detention Center.

DID YOU KNOW?

Gun violence in Birmingham, Alabama, has been a significant and escalating concern in recent years. Here's an overview of the current statistics and trends:

Recent Statistics: Alabama Reporter

- Homicide Rates: In 2022, Birmingham recorded 144 homicides, marking the deadliest year in recent memory and surpassing the previous high of 141 homicides in 1991.
- 2023 Trends: The city experienced a slight reduction in homicides, with 135 recorded, breaking a five-year trend of increasing violent killings.
- 2024 Surge: As of November 2024, Birmingham's homicide count has exceeded the total for 2023, indicating a resurgence in lethal violence

Contributing Factors

- Firearm Accessibility: The prevalence of firearms, including illegal modifications like "Glock switches" that enable fully automatic firing, has exacerbated the lethality of violent incidents.
- Socioeconomic Challenges: Economic disparities and historical social injustices contribute to the underlying causes of violence in the city.

Recent Incidents

- Mass Shootings: In September 2024, a mass shooting outside a popular hookah bar resulted in four deaths and 17 injuries, marking the city's third quadruple homicide of the year.

Comparative Analysis

- National Context: Birmingham's homicide rate is among the highest in the United States, with a violent crime rate of 1,682 per 100,000 residents and a property crime rate of 4,173 per 100,000 residents.

Community Impact

- Public Perception: The surge in violence has led to increased fear and concern among residents, with community leaders calling for comprehensive strategies to address the crisis.

Efforts to Address Gun Violence

- Law Enforcement Initiatives: The Birmingham Police Department has implemented various strategies to curb gun violence, including public service announcements and community engagement efforts.
- Community Programs: Local organizations are working to address the root causes of violence through economic development, education, and social services.

Conclusion: Birmingham continues to grapple with high levels of gun violence, with recent statistics indicating a troubling resurgence in homicides. Addressing this issue requires a multifaceted approach, including law enforcement efforts, community engagement, and addressing underlying socioeconomic factors.

CHAPTER 11
"MEETING THE FAMILY"

If anyone fails to provide for his own, and especially for those of his own family, he has denied the faith [by disregarding its precepts] and is worse than an unbeliever [who fulfills his obligation in these matters].
1 Timothy 5:8

"To profess faith in Christ while refusing to care for those in need, especially one's own relatives, is to show a 'dead' faith; essentially denying the faith and showing oneself to be less virtuous than an unbeliever."

Months went by and now it's 2015 and Aron is getting out of the Juvenile Detention Center towards the end of summer. We were hoping that he had learned from that place and had come to his senses. Well not long after being released, he asked for a ride to go over to his friend's house. We took him over there and he told us I'll be home later. That later turned into days for him not coming home which resulted in him cutting school. My wife and I looked at one another and said to ourselves "Maybe if we take him with us to meet the family in Florida just maybe this might help him to see the bigger picture in Life." We sent the word to family members who might have seen him on the neighborhood block to tell him about the trip. So word got back to him and he responded to the message, he came home. Thanksgiving of 2015 is when we visit the family in Tampa, Florida where he could meet his brother and sisters (by marriage).

We made it to Florida, which was his first time in a Southern State. There were things in Florida he had never seen before. There were times he would tell Momma V, "Those trees ain't real there is no way these trees are perfectly planted." Momma V stopped the car and told him to get out and take a leaf off the tree, he did and was amazed. There was a time when we went shopping at Brandon Mall and my son wanted some things, my wife and I looked at one another and told him, "Now if you do right by us by doing right in school we will get you anything you want but as of now NO!" He felt some type of way about that and he mumbled some things under his breath. We were enjoying our family in Florida and everybody had a GREAT time the four days we were in Florida.

Now we made it back to Louisville, Kentucky. It was time for school and I took him to school that morning. While on the way to school, I was talking to him about the promise he will do this and promised me you will do that, etc. He agreed as usual and I dropped him off at school. Now it is around the time he gets home from school at 2:45 pm and he didn't come home. When my wife (Valerie J. Ware) came home from school she asked "Where is Aron?" I looked at her and said, "He didn't come home." She looked at me and said, "I told you he would do this when we get back." I just shook my head and said, "Here we go again."

At this point in his life, he decided to run the streets. Shortly after that, we got a phone call from the Detention Center in Jeffersonville, Indiana where he got caught breaking into a car my son was 16 and about to turn 17 years old.

CHAPTER 12

"MENACE TO SOCIETY"

Galatians 5:13

[13] For you, my brothers, were called to freedom; only do not let your freedom become an opportunity for the sinful nature (worldliness, selfishness), but through love serve and seek the best for one another.

"Menacing behavior is expressing or showing an intention to inflict, or threatening to inflict, harm or injury upon someone or something."

It's the year 2016, Aron is 17 years old and in Boot Camp (Juvenile penitentiary) in Kokomo, Indiana where he was doing 6 months, from December 2015 to June 2016. In between times, we had moved to Turtle Creek Apts in Louisville, Kentucky. Aron was in Boot Camp where he had achieved his High School Diploma and he mailed it home before he got out of Boot Camp. We were so PROUD of him for getting his education while in boot camp and not losing focus. Six months had passed and now it's the month of June.

We heard the knock at the door, I answered the door and our son surprised us, he was standing there with a BIG smile on his face. Momma V was standing behind me with a smile on her face and we embraced him with love. We said, "WELCOME HOME!" we were so proud of him. He stayed a couple of nights at our apartment. One day he asked if I could take him over to Grandma's house (my mother) and I did take him.

I remember telling him when he was younger, "When you complete school and turn 18 years old, I am going to treat you with respect as an adult." So we arrived at my mother's house. He got out and said, “I'll be home in a little bit.” That little bit turned into days and days turned into months. He decided to hang out with his so-called "Bros" (Childhood friends), where he became a menace to society. He never came back home, he was just hanging out in the streets. I would get calls from family members saying, "I just seen Aron out there," or "I just seen Aron doing this & that," etc.

I would call his phone and tell him, “I didn't raise you like this!” It was going in one ear out the other. At this point, Aron's mind was made up in what he wanted to do and what he wanted to be involved in. Now my biggest fear as a father was coming slowly but surely to reality something was happening to him. My Wife, aka “Momma V” and I would put him before the LORD (in prayer) every day. "Lord cover and protect our son Aron, wherever he may be in Jesus' name, Amen." A couple of months has passed and it is now the month of December. We heard a knock at the door I answered and there was our son, Aron with two of his childhood friends. We welcomed him home and welcomed his friends as well. They didn't stay too long but the strangest thing happened. Our son, Aron begin to show his friends around our apartment. We had pictures hanging on the wall and he began to explain to his friends who was what and what this meant to him.

His diploma was on the wall and he began to boast and brag to his friends about getting their education like he did. He said, "Stay in school and get your diploma like I did." They stayed a little while longer. We all talked and laughed about things. I started telling his friends about GOD, and we had a great conversation. However, one of his friends, the whole while, seemed a little bit at ease. As a father, I was observing and discerning but I didn't bother him. Our son, Aron got up and said, "Ok, Pops and Momma V, we are heading out. I rose with them as they were getting ready to go!"

They said their goodbyes and we said, "NO! See you later no goodbyes." He looked and smiled and walked out the door. That was the last time we had seen him that year.

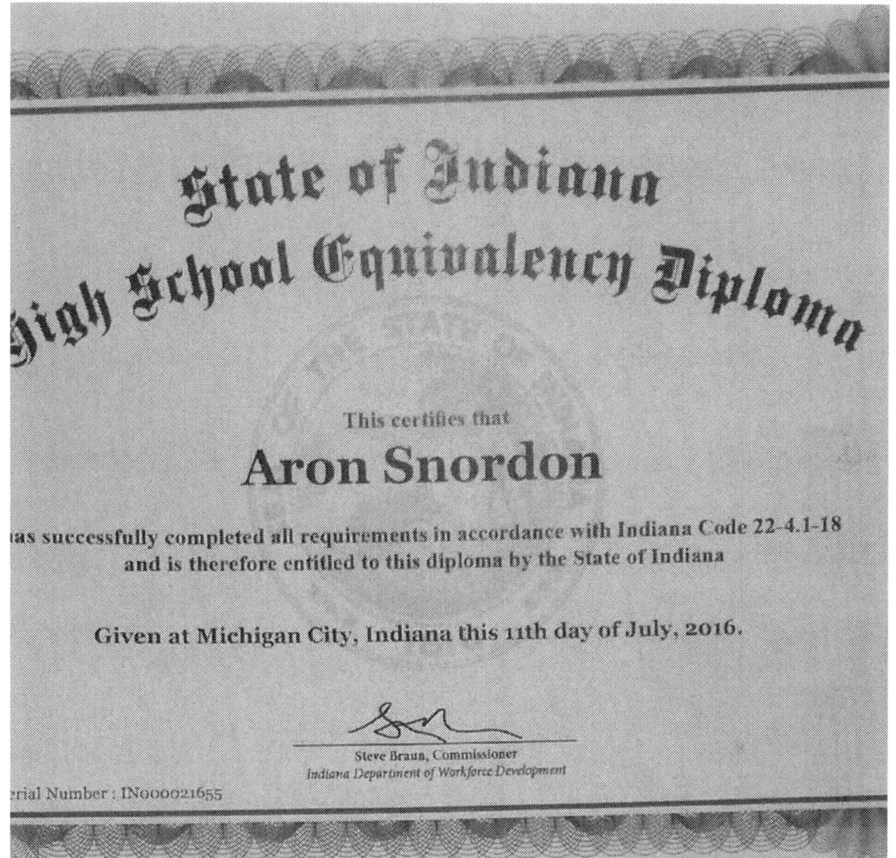

State of Indiana

igh School Equivalency Diploma

This certifies that

Aron Snordon

as successfully completed all requirements in accordance with Indiana Code 22-4.1-18
and is therefore entitled to this diploma by the State of Indiana

Given at Michigan City, Indiana this 11th day of July, 2016.

Steve Braun, Commissioner
Indiana Department of Workforce Development

rial Number : IN000021655

CHAPTER 13

"THE TROUBLE ROAD"

Matthew 7:13-14

[13] "Enter through the narrow gate. For wide is the gate and broad and easy to travel is the path that leads the way to destruction and eternal loss, and there are many who enter through it. [14] But small is the gate and narrow and difficult to travel is the path that leads the way to [everlasting] life, and there are few who find it.

The wide gate of the world promises life and happiness but delivers destruction. The way of Christ requires that we lay our lives down, but in that sacrifice, we find a reward of life. Sadly, the gate that is wide and the way that is broad is the one most people travel. That way leads to destruction.

The year is now 2017, Aron was 17 going on 18 and his birthday was fast approaching (February 11). Donald Trump won the election and will become the President of the United States. In a couple of days, we will be into the new year. On January 5, 2017, between 8 to 8:30 pm, I received a phone call from my son's Godfather. I answered "Hello what's up?"

He replied, "Man it's about your son he is here he wants to tell you something."

I replied, "Put him on the phone." Aron got on the phone crying he replied "Daddy! Daddy! PLEASE PRAY FOR ME!" He was crying and telling me what had happened. I begin to pray for him and pray for that situation asking GOD to fix it. Bring peace and healing to the situation. GOD came in and touched him and that

Shortly after the phone call we had received, we were watching the news about the situation Aron was telling us about that occurred. A shooting at a gas station in New Albany, Indiana. Sources say that Aron had got a ride to a certain destination point at a gas station off Charleston Road in New Albany, Indiana. An argument had occurred in the vehicle between an individual and Aron. The driver began to tell them to get out as Aron and the other individual were leaving the vehicle. The driver began to take off as they were stepping out of the vehicle and the other individual had got trapped between inside and outside the door. Aron began to panic. He grabbed his firearm and fired shots at the vehicle to try to stop the vehicle.

The passenger in the vehicle got injured with a non-life-threatening injury. Aron then began to panic more, and he left the scene on foot...... Now as a father, I was very disappointed at this point. Some days afterward, while I was at work, my wife "Momma V" called. I answered and replied "Hey Baby!" She replied "The police are here, searching our home!" She put the police on the phone and he began to explain why and what is going on. Aron was involved in a shooting. He began to ask questions like, "Where is your son?" etc., I replied, "I have no idea where he may be".

At this point, Momma V and I were so embarrassed and ashamed. I got off work and immediately headed home to see what was going on. My wife explained everything to me that the cops had told her and they had left a card for me to call them when and if he arrives. They wanted me to talk to him to turn himself in. So we waited for his call or hoped that he would show up. He never called because he didn't have a phone at the time as far as we knew. Two months passed, and it was springtime, around March. I started a new job at Victory Packaging Warehouse work driving forklifts. On March 16, 2017, I got a phone call from his Godfather.

I answered, "Hey What's up."

He replied "Bro! They arrested your son, I'm here now."

The police had a standoff with the guy in the house and had their guns out ready to shoot. Your son called me crying scared for his life thinking that the police were going to shoot the house up. I immediately got the police's attention and told them what Aron said so they put their guns down after I told them. Bro, I talked them boys into surrendering."

I replied, "WHAT! WOW!"

He replied, "Yeah man I know!"

So I just listened to him on the phone. I called my wife and told her the news. We both were sad about everything that happened from the phone call, which happened on Bolling Ave in Louisville, KY. Now months had passed and our son was in and out of the courtroom in downtown New Albany, Indiana. My wife and I had to be in court to testify on his behalf. This was the final court appearance. I testified and told them about our son, where he came from and what he and I have been through, etc. Then the strangest thing happened, A quick recess was requested. His lawyer told us he will be giving us a call soon. This soon turned into hours, hours into days, days into months.

It dawned on us and we realized that Aron ain't getting out any time soon so we gave it to the Lord in prayer. We finally found out that they were going to give him 36 years, "BUT GOD!" God touched that situation. Instead of 36 years, they gave him two years and six months in prison. God showed his mercy in that situation on our son's behalf. I visited him, we talked and prayed until they sent him off to prison between Kokomo, & South Bend, Indiana, where he had to do his time for his crime.

CHAPTER 14
"MISSED TIME"
(2017 - 2019)

Ephesians 5:16-17
[16] making the very most of your time [on earth, recognizing and taking advantage of each opportunity and using it with wisdom and diligence], because the days are [filled with] evil. [17] Therefore do not be foolish and thoughtless, but understand and firmly grasp what the will of the Lord is.

In essence, He's instructing us, to "maximize each moment" by taking advantage of every opportunity God gives us. Allow Jesus to be our role model for keeping a balanced schedule. He knew that spending time with the Father was the most important thing he could do.

Time is a precious resource given to us by God, and how we use it matters. In this fast-paced world it's easy to get caught up in distractions and activities that don't align with our purpose.

BOXING ACADEM

LB

In Loving Memory Of
Juan E. Clay
Sunrise: April 9,
April 7, 2018
Service
Friday, April 13, 2018
11:00 A.M.
Greater St. Mark

All
you need
is
Love
He
Has
Risen!

All
you need
is
Love

40

CHAPTER 15
"BACK HOME"

Luke 15:17-20

[17] But when he [finally] came to his senses, he said, 'How many of my father's hired men have more than enough food, while I am dying here of hunger! [18] I will get up and go to my father, and I will say to him, "Father, I have sinned against heaven and in your sight. [19] I am no longer worthy to be called your son; [just] treat me like one of your hired men." ' [20] So he got up and came to his father. But while he was still a long way off, his father saw him and was moved with compassion for him, and ran and embraced him and kissed him.

The story of the prodigal son is a picture of God's love for us as His children. God's love for us does not depend on our faithfulness; it is unconditional. He loved us while we were still sinners. Though we are demanding and do not remain faithful, God is still our faithful and loving Father.

The year is 2019, we have moved from living in a two-bedroom apartment into a two-bedroom house. During 2017 and 2019 there were a lot of changes and challenges with jobs and life situations but God made a way for us to move in the year of 2019. In July 2019, I am now a worker at Coca-Cola Warehouse. About the 3rd week of July, we got a phone call from his Godfather (my brother). I answered "Hello what's up Bro?"

He replied "Bro I got some good news. Your son just got out and he is on his way to you as we speak. Don't tell him I told y'all because it's supposed to be a surprise." I replied, "WHAT! HE IS OUT?" He replied, "Yes Bro he is out Bro!" We talked for a little bit about some things and got off the phone with excitement and enthusiasm. My wife and I are waiting for his arrival with anticipation.

Now two hours have gone by, and we get a knock at the door, I answered, and it was him, our Son Aron T. Snordon. We just loved on him and welcomed him with open arms, "WELCOME BACK HOME."

See, through prayer, God worked a miracle in his life for that shooting back in 2017. He was facing 30 years because one of the bullets went through a government official's home. Luckily no one was injured and because of lack of evidence, the judge dropped the 30 years sentence to 2 1/2 years in the penitentiary, with 3 years of probation (strict probation with no trouble). If he got into any trouble within 3 years he had 15 years over his head. The crazy thing is that Aron didn't do any outstanding crime in Louisville, maybe a couple of minor misdemeanors and incidents here and there but not major. His serious charges were over in the New Albany, Indiana side, their laws are different than Kentucky laws. You have to serve out your time there in Kentucky, one year is six months of serve time. In 2016, Donald Trump was the President, the government signed and passed the reconsidering of the right to bear arms bill.

On Feb. 4, 2016, In a campaign video released on Facebook, Trump posted bluntly, “I won’t let them take away our guns!”. Gun violence increased dramatically, it got into the wrong hands of people. Nevertheless, Aron was fresh out starting to begin his new chapter in life trying to adjust from being incarcerated to being out (free). He was staying with us for a few weeks when he decided to go and again stay over at a friend's place. He picked up his things and left. We just told him to "be careful and we are praying for you" he said Love y'all and thanks.

A couple of months passed, and Aron would call us at times and send pictures letting us know his "whereabouts" hanging out with old friends. It's the beginning week of November before Thanksgiving of 2019 our daughter received a phone call saying "Aron got Shot! He is on his way to the hospital!" She hung up the phone, ran to the living room shouting, "ARON JUST GOT SHOT! HE IS ON HIS WAY! WE NEED TO GET TO THE HOSPITAL!" ASAP!"

We were in shock and speechless, we didn't waste any time. We jumped into our car heading towards U of L Hospital. We got to the hospital, and arrived in the waiting room with friends and family trying to get information on what, when, and how this happened. Aron and other sources told me what happened that day. That was weeks prior before the shooting.

The neighbor next door confronted them about trash being in their yard, this was an ongoing conflict. On this particular day, Aron happens to be over there so earlier that morning, the neighbor next door knocked on the door. Aron answered the door, they exchanged words peacefully and Aron went back to Bed. Two hours later Aron woke up and went to the store, as he was heading to the store his girlfriend at that time called him, "Aron, come get this dude!" Aron began to run back to the house, the neighbor and his girlfriend were arguing outside on the porch. Aron approached the neighbor for her safety and he then began to have a conversation with the neighbor.

The neighbor said something that provoked Aron and he got so upset at the neighbor, knocking the phone out of the neighbor's hand. Aron then told everyone on the porch to get back into the house, about 10 seconds after they began to walk inside the house about five shots were fired at them. As they ran into the house one bullet hit Aron in the back causing him to fall in the doorway. That one shot temporarily paralyzed him from the waist down so Aron began to crawl towards the back to get his gun to protect them.

Aron began to fire shots back at the door to scare the guy away from them. This was the information that was told to me about that situation. Aron stayed in the hospital for about two weeks within that time he began to have feelings in his lower body and his legs. Shortly after this, he was healed enough to begin therapy treatments which was a success. During this time so many people (Friends, Family, and Saints)would come and visit him and spend time with him. Shortly after this his Godfather and Godmother took him out of Lagrange, Kentucky (out of Prospect) where he was protected and where he could fully recover from his wound. "THE POWER OF PRAYER!" WOW!!! Christ requires that we lay our lives down, but in that sacrifice, we find a reward of life. Sadly, the gate that is wide and the way that is broad is the one most people travel. That way leads to destruction.

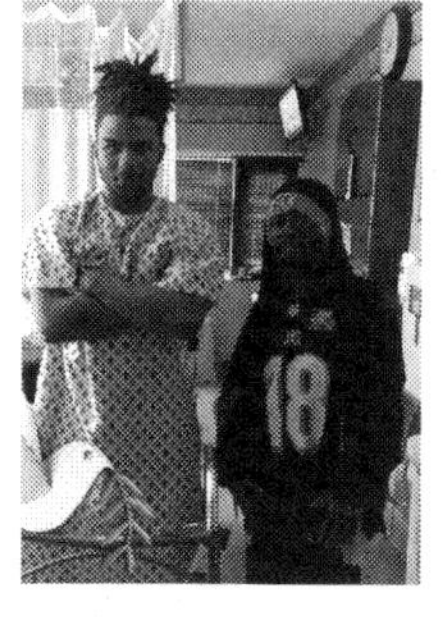
18

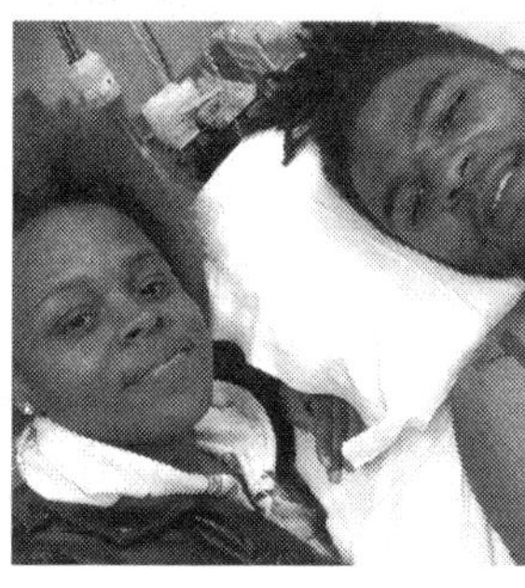

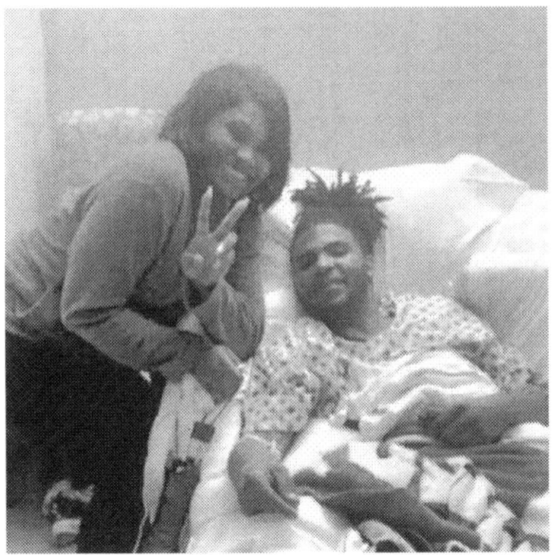

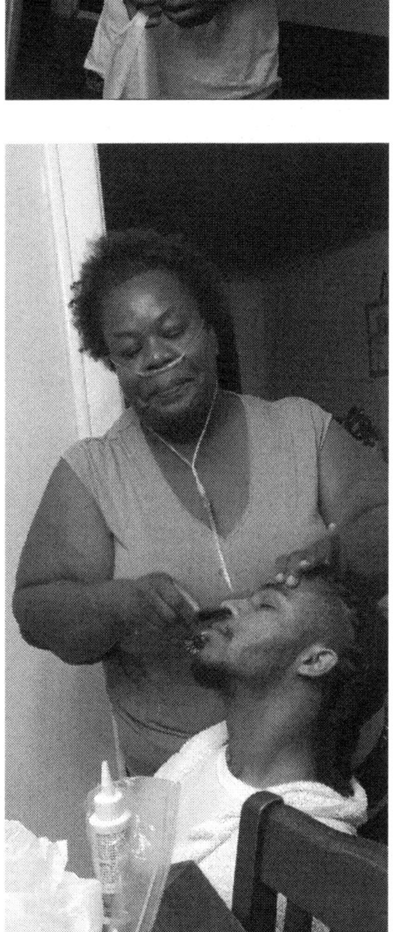

CHAPTER 16

"THE E-TOWN RIDE OF REDEMPTION" (The Year Of COVID-19)"

Matthew 6:14-15
[14] For if you forgive others their trespasses [their reckless and willful sins], your heavenly Father will also forgive you.
[15] But if you do not forgive others [nurturing your hurt and anger with the result that it interferes with your relationship with God], then your Father will not forgive your trespasses.

Unforgiveness will produce bitterness. Bitterness can be directly traced to the failure to forgive. It makes you caustic, condemning, and nasty. Harassed by the memories of what you can't forgive, your thoughts become malignant toward others, and your whole view of life becomes distorted. The negative consequences of not forgiving have been documented in studies that show that it can lead to the emotional pain of anger, hate, hurt, resentment, bitterness, etc. and as a consequence can create health issues, affect relationships, and stop us from experiencing the freedom that forgiveness enables.

It's now 2020, and Aron's birthday has passed (February 11) he is now 21 years old. It's now the month of March 2020 we have not seen him since after he got shot and was in the hospital. I remember when our Pastor came and visited Aron in the hospital, he prayed for him and told him what the LORD said to him about his life.

He needed to get back in church and I remember looking at our son, he had tears in his eyes as the Pastor talked to him. My son received what the Pastor said because two months afterward, he surprised everyone and showed up to church. Now a month after he came to church on this particular day I received a phone call before I had to ride out to Elizabeth, Kentucky (E-Town). I had to take something out to my little brother's house. I answered the phone and said, "Hello what's up." He replied, "Hey Pop what's up, what you doing?" I replied, "Oh nothing about to run out your uncle's place out in E-Town to take him something, what's up?" He replied, "Can I roll? ... can you come Scoop me?" I replied, "Yeah sure, tell me where you at?"

So he told me where his location was and I rolled up and he got in the car. The ride to E-Town was a 45-minute ride from Louisville I-65 South. The ride was quiet for about 15 minutes, so I asked, "What's up?...you are quiet...what's up?" He replied, "Yeah pop I need to talk to you about something glad you asked". I replied, "Yeah what's up" he replied, "Cool", he began to talk to me about everything. He was crying from when he was younger and how I treated him like an outcast. And how it made him feel like I wasn't his son, etc... so as he was talking I interrupted him, and he said, "See right there, that is what I'm talking about you always cut me off and don't listen to me!" So right before I was going to replied the Lord spoke to me and said "Listen to him", so I listened to him. In fact I listened to him the whole time for about 30 minutes.

So when he got done talking the Lord spoke to me again and said, "Ask for his forgiveness and you forgive him as well."

I replied, "Son I didn't know that you felt that way, can you forgive me?". He responded, "See I always wanted you to listen to me, and yes Pop, I forgive you." I replied, "Son I love man" He responded, "I love you too, Pop." We made it to my brother's place and took care of business with him for my mother. We spent a couple of hours there in E-Town with my brother.

On the way back home my son and I bonded. I remember telling him, "Aron, listen to me, now we got that clear. You are a grown man and I will not treat you like you are a baby anymore. From here on out, I'm going to respect you and treat you as an adult" He responded, "Cool that's what up Pop."

So we laughed and talk about all the things we had been through together, a great conversation. We have made it back to the city (Louisville). I took him back over to his friend's place, and his response was, "Alright Pop I see you later."

I responded, "Cool be careful out here and I see you."
We both told each other "Love you."

I arrived back home and told my wife about everything we talked about and how GOD came right on in and reconciled our relationship.

My Wife responded, "WOW! Look at GOD...to GOD be the Glory!"

I said, "Amen". March going into April the world got a big shake-up with "COVID-19" which was spreading all over the world. Everybody is wearing masks this was the year that Joe Biden became President of the United States of America.

First year in office this plague took out so many family members and friends. This was a very scary year, my mother was in and out of the hospital around this time and it was hard to visit loved ones in the hospital because of COVID-19. We would take turns on visiting, I would go days then our son would go one day off and on.

This went on for a couple of weeks until they sent momma to a Rehab Facility where she had to stay there for about one month. Momma finally came home, she had stopped smoking cigarettes to recover her health and her strength back.

It's the month of May, Mother's Day had passed. The month of June is "summertime" and it's the month of Father's Day. Our son and daughter (his sister by marriage) surprised me by coming over for Father's Day.

They gave me cards and gifts, I was the HAPPIEST MAN ON EARTH! I was smiling from ear to ear and so proud. We had already invited friends and family over before they surprised me and lit up Father's Day. After this many more surprises came on the 4th of July, my birthday surprise, and our daughter was pregnant with our grandson. My two favorite moments that year were my surprise birthday party that our son, my wife, and our daughter set up for me. Aron had surprised me with a kitten, he knows I love cats and our daughter was pregnant with our grandson. That year I was the Head Coach for the California Jets Mighty Mites Division ages 5-7. Our two granddaughters were cheerleading that season. Everything was going so perfectly that year despite COVID-19 being on the rise. It was going well for our family.

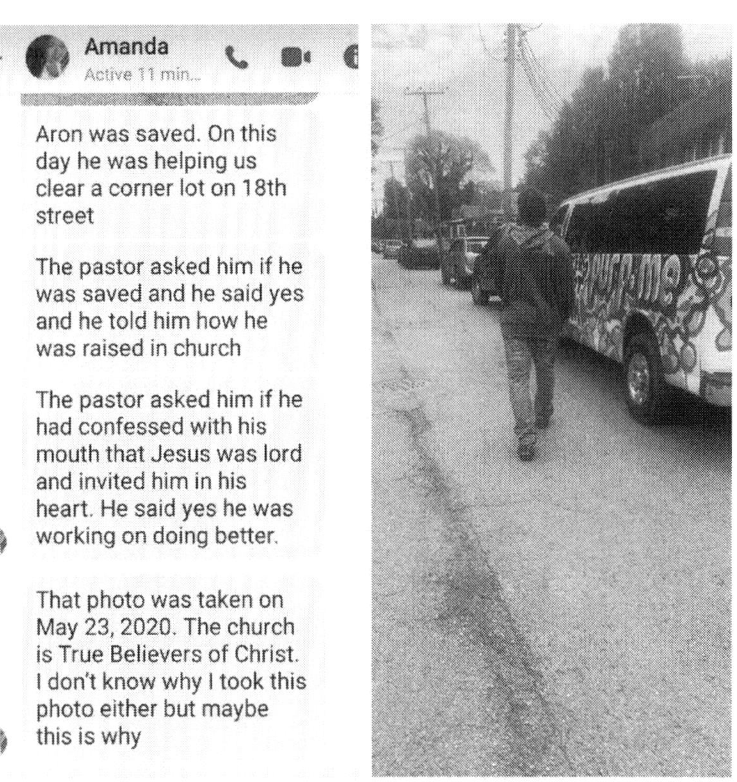

6504

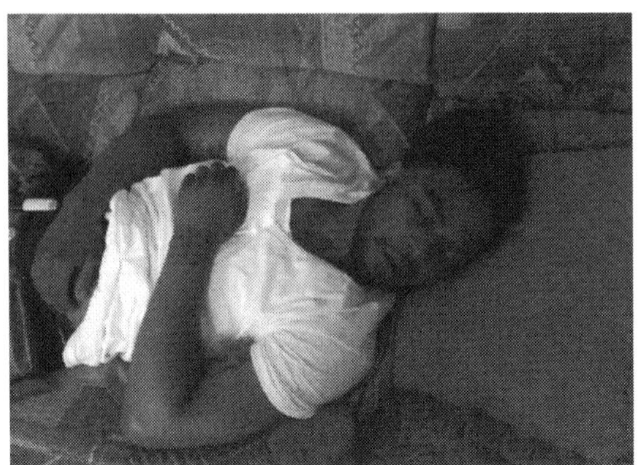

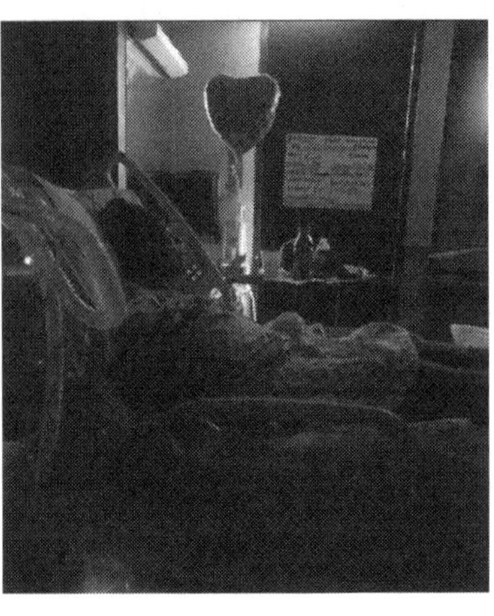

CHAPTER 17
"THE YEAR OF WARNING"

Proverbs 16:18-20
[18] Pride goes before destruction, And a haughty spirit before a fall. [19] It is better to be humble in spirit with the lowly Than to divide the spoil with the proud (haughty, arrogant). [20] He who pays attention to the word [of God] will find good, And blessed (happy, prosperous, to be admired) is he who trusts [confidently] in the Lord.

Pride goes before destruction, a haughty spirit before a fall. Better to be lowly in spirit along with the oppressed than to share plunder with the proud. Whoever gives heed to instruction prospers, and blessed is the one who trusts in the LORD. This often-cited proverb notes that arrogance puts a person at risk for disaster. As with many such statements, it is true in both physical and spiritual ways. Overestimating one's athletic skills might result in severe injury. "Cocky" fighters—those who become too self-confident—might suffer a stunning upset.

In the year 2021 our Pastor at this time had got a Word from the Lord. He told us, "Thus said the Lord", for everyone to get a notebook and write your family & close friends names down. Next to their names write what you want God to do for them. After that anointed it with bless oil draw a Cross over the paper and bless your homes", so we received that word from our Pastor.

This was around the first month of that year the time of our month of fasting and consecration. It's now the month of February, and the fasting and praying have ended this year. Tampa Bay was Hosting the 53rd SUPERBOWL which the Buccaneers were in. My wife and I flew to Tampa, and the Buccs won their 2nd SUPERBOWL. Two weeks after that our daughter had our grandson February 20, 2021, Aron's nephew. We were so excited he made our 10th Grandchild.

During March, April, May, and June our son would pop up in different cars and sometimes with different females. He mostly loved to be around his sister who he loved dearly they were very very close but this particular day our son and a female friend came over and Momma V (my Wife) was always cooking something. When they find out Momma V is cooking they come rushing over lol in a heartbeat... Nevertheless.

On this day later on that night Aron said "Daddy come out on the porch with me" I said "Ok" so we got on the porch and he began to talk and told me EVERYTHING!! I mean EVERYTHING!

What happened over the past months earlier that year in January, he told me about a fight he had with his girlfriend's friend's father. His girlfriend liked the other girl but the father did not agree with his daughter liking another girl. On that day in January, Aron told me his girlfriend called him and told him that her father was all in her face so being her friend, he went over there to try to bring peace.

However, Aron told me that the guy tried to take it out on him. Our son said he had to defend himself so they fought and Aron got the best of him. So as I'm listening to him tell me all these events I just shook my head.

Unfortunately, some of the family members of the guy he fought and won are now mad at him. Another situation he told me about was a married woman he was secretly involved with. When I heard this the Lord began to minister to me to minister to him.

So after he told me all these stories, I replied, "You sure you don't have a price over your head?" He replied laughing, "Naw Pops I'm good in the city. I'm so real out here! Everybody loves me. Pops, I'm GOOD!"

Later in our Conversation God pressed it on my heart to minister to him I said to him "Don't you see ..... the devil is trying his best to trap you like a mouse."

After I had told him this, he pondered on it...and then he began telling me other things that were going on with him. As I was listening I was concerned about his whereabouts. I remember him telling me about when every time his friends would call him, he was "Johnny-on-the-spot" but when it came to him everyone was slow to come through for him. When he shared that with me I got sad but one thing about my son, he really didn't want people to feel sorry for him. I encouraged him that GOD still loved him and he was waiting on him and he replied, "I know Pops."

Hours passed by, and we started talking about 9 pm that night, and we didn't finish talking until about 3 am. That was a father-and-son moment we had that night, we were laughing and talking. I really enjoyed our time together but one thing I won't ever forget about that night. He looked at me and said "Pops that was the realist advice you ever told me, I'm going to listen to that and act on that...nobody told it like you did Pops". He did what the Lord told me to tell him for a short time before the devil temptation came along. I started seeing his behaviors had changed, he stopped coming around and he would call us here and there.

One day I asked my wife why she thought he was acting like this her reply was, "Aron had come across a money flip organization where he applied for and got the loan, a nice amount of money". I asked "What is he doing with the money?" She replied, "I don't know". So now it's Mother's Day, Aron didn't come over but he did call my wife and told her "Happy Mother's Day Momma V", and told her he was spending time with his mother, she replied, "That is ok."

After days and weeks passed by, he would call and pop up now and then. It was Father's Day, and Aron had come over earlier that day to spend time with Momma V and his sister. They began to ask him questions like why and what was going on. He answered the questions they asked him. Later after I got off work, it was just my Wife and our daughter but not Aron. He did leave me a Louisville Cardinals shirt and a card. I began to get upset about why his behavior was changing all of a sudden with me...my wife answered and said, He told us "he was mad at you about the past." I replied, "I thought we squash that stuff", she replied, "Apparently not". Our daughter said that she told him, "At the end of the day, still get your daddy something to show him you appreciate him." Aron looked and said, "True". From that day on his attitude was changing, something that we were trying to figure out which was a very big concern.

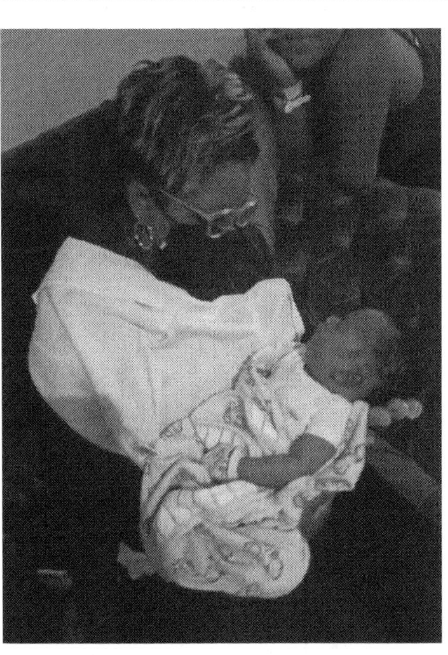

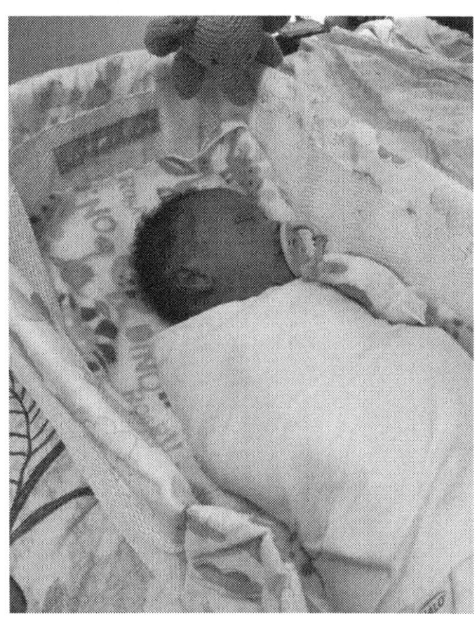

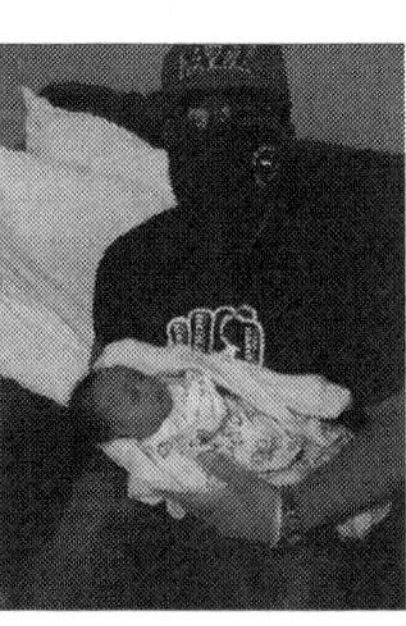

PARENTAL
ADVISORY
EXPLICIT CONTENT

2021
Happy New Year

saying, What shall we eat? or,
What shall we drink? or, Where-
withal shall we be clothed?
32 (For after all these things
do the Gentiles seek:) for your
heavenly Father knoweth that
ye have need of all these things.
33 But seek ye first the kingdom
of God, and his righteousness;
and all these things shall be
added unto you.
34 Take therefore no thought
for the morrow: for the morrow
shall take thought for the things
of itself. Sufficient unto the day
is the evil thereof.

CHAPTER 7

JUDGE not, that ye be not
judged.
2 For with what judgment ye
judge, ye shall be judged: and
with what measure ye mete, it
shall be measured to you again.
3 And why beholdest thou the
mote that is in thy brother's eye,
but considerest not the beam
that is in thine own eye?
4 Or how wilt thou say to thy
brother, Let me pull out the mote
out of thine eye; and, behold, a
beam *is* in thine own eye?
5 Thou hypocrite, first cast out
the beam out of thine own eye;
and then shalt thou see clearly
to cast out the mote out of thy
brother's eye.
6 ¶ Give not that which is holy
unto the dogs, neither cast ye
your pearls before swine, lest
they trample them under their
feet, and turn again and rend you.

7 ¶ Ask, and it shall be g
you; seek, and ye shall f
knock, and it shall be opened
to you:
8 For every one that ask
ceiveth; and he that seeket
eth; and to him that knoc
shall be opened.
9 Or what man is there of y
whom if his son ask bread, wil
give him a stone?
10 Or if he ask a fish, will he g
him a serpent?
11 If ye then, being evil, k
how to give good gifts unto y
children, how much more sh
your Father which is in hea
give good things to them tha
him?
12 Therefore all things wh
ever ye would that men sh
do to you, do ye even so to t
for this is the law and the p
ets.
13 ¶ Enter ye in at the
gate: for wide *is* the gate
broad *is* the way, that leade
destruction, and many the
which go in thereat:
14 Because strait *is* the gate
narrow *is* the way, which le
unto life, and few there b
find it.
15 ¶ Beware of false pro
which come to you in
clothing, but inwardly t
ravening wolves.
16 Ye shall know them b
fruits. Do men gather g
thorns, or figs of thistles?
17 Even so every goo
bringeth forth good fruit;

(Momma) Mary Patterson – Healing, Miracle
(Bro) Micheal Ware – Salvation Deliverance
(Bro) Sonny Ware – Salvation Deliverance
(Sis) Tracy Jones – Salvation Deliverance
(Sis) Lisa Ware – Salvation Deliverance
(Bro) Leon Ware – Salvation Deliverance
My Nieces and Nephews – Salvation
Deliverance
My close cousins that I know –
Salvation Deliverance
All our Grandchildren – Salvation Deliverance
All our Children Erica, Maurice,
Keisha, Stacy, Dajzah, Aron –
Salvation Deliverance
All our close Friends – Salvation Deliverance
Me and Wife – Deliverance from old
Sinnful Habits

I CAN DO EVERYTHING THROUGH CHRIST
WHO GIVES ME STRENGTH. PHIL 4:13

Valerie J Ware

Steelers
Steelers
NFL

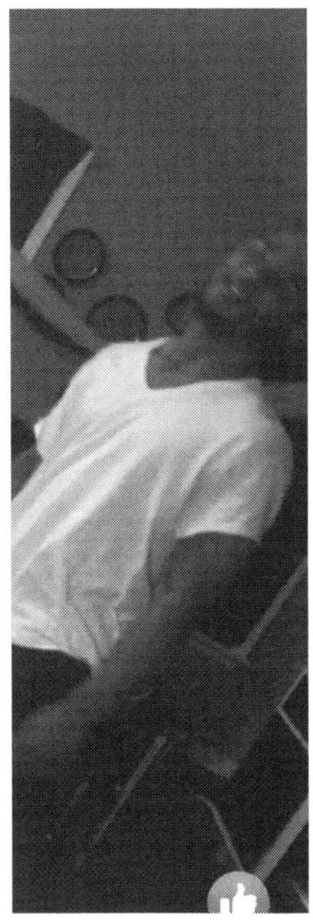

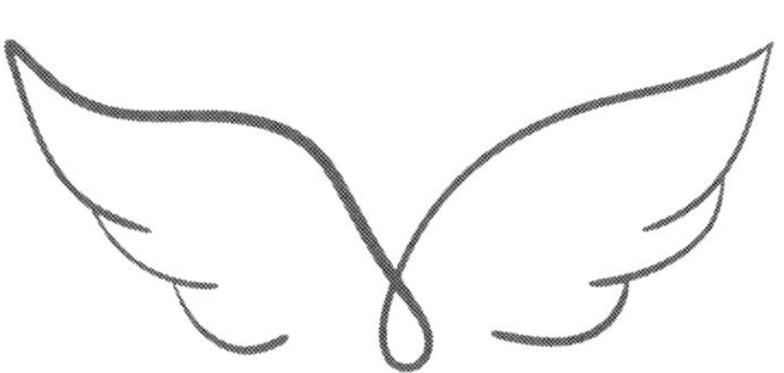

CHAPTER 18
"THE DAY OF 8/22"

Romans 8:22-23

[22] For we know that the whole creation has been moaning together as in the pains of childbirth until now. [23] And not only this, but we too, who have the first fruits of the Spirit [a joyful indication of the blessings to come], even we groan inwardly, as we wait eagerly for [the sign of] our adoption as sons—the redemption and transformation of our body [at the resurrection].

In Romans 8:22-23, Paul uses an interesting, memorable, and striking metaphor. Presently the whole creation, he says, groans in labor pains; its condition is like a woman giving birth to a child. Something is about to happen, an outcome. But for now, there is a waiting. In God's timing, the entire creation will share what Christians have now — adoption by God and transformation into a new status, redemption. The phrase "redemption of our bodies" signifies an eschatological renewal of ourselves in our totality, including our bodily existence.

In Romans 8:23 he says we have the "first fruits of the Spirit." The Greek term for "first fruits" (aparche) is a cultic one, used in both pagan Greek sources and in the Septuagint (Exodus 23:19; 25:2-3; Leviticus 22:12), referring to either agricultural produce or animals presented to God and consecrated before the rest of a crop or herd could be put to use.

In the present context, Paul is saying that believers have already the first installment of what is to come. They experience proleptically that which is in store for the entire creation.

Now, it is the 4th of July 2021, we called Aron, but he did not answer and we have received no text messages from him. He just wasn't acting like himself and as a Father, I was concerned and a little upset and disappointed at him. I was wondering all night while the fireworks bursting in the sky if the neighbors next door were popping their guns as the celebration was going on. I'm waiting to hear from him but he never called or texted. It was about 3 am on July 5th, everyone was heading home.

While we were heading home, I said to my wife "Why did he never text back I hope he is good", my wife said, "Keep him in prayer". So later on that week, my wife told me about this money he had gotten, which I forgot about. I was getting in my feelings and I went to the phone store and asked them to cut the other phone line off which they did. When I got home I told my wife what I did, she asked, "Why?" I replied, "Because he didn't come through on Father's Day...he didn't come over on Mother's Day. I'm upset and he got this so call money, he needed to own up to his responsibilities." My Wife replied, "Don't do it...keep his phone on." I replied, "Naw he didn't come through on Father's Day." However, when I think about it now I should have listened to my wife. I didn't know one of these days it was going to backfire on me for being selfish in my feelings.

It's August 9, 2021, it's my birthday and Aron didn't show up. I was sad deep inside. At this point, I couldn't figure out why Aron was acting this way. Only my wife, our daughter and her son, and our daughter's boyfriend (our Future Son-in-law) was there for my birthday. We had a wonderful time celebrating my 43rd birthday. A day after my birthday, I get a text message from our son Aron, "So we on this now Pops"...I replied, "On what?" He texted back, "You cut my phone off." I replied, "Yes, you have to be responsible.

You have to pay your bill." He texted back, "Nevermind, it's cool" and that was the last conversation I had before that horrible day, 13 days later.

On August 21, 2021, I had a football game out of town I had to coach against the Franklin County Rams that we got cheated out of. I was having a bad weekend. On Sunday, August 22, 2021, I worked from 7 am to 7 pm. I remember getting off work that day just drained from Saturday and from working all that day. I came home and our daughter and grandchildren was at the house. I remember the little ones asking me, "Paw Paw can you play the game with us?" I told them "Paw Paw is very very tired maybe next time." This was around 7:25 pm and our daughter and grandchildren had left. I remembered lying down so exhausted from the weekend.

I got a phone call from my little brother's wife at approximately 8:06 pm I asked, "What's up"...she replied, crying and hysterical, "ARON BEEN SHOT LAYING IN BLOOD!" I responded, "WHAT!..HERE!", her respond was, "OVER THERE, ON GREENWOOD!" I got off the phone in a RAGE! I turned around and told my wife, "ARON GOT SHOT LAYING IN A POOL OF BLOOD!" My Wife replied, "OH MY GOD, WHAT!" So we jumped up, got in the car and headed there.

I remember the ride was in slow motion even though we were going 70mph, but it felt like we were going 45mph. It felt like the movie "BOYS IN THE HOOD", the part when he scream "RICKY!" that slow motion. When we got there to the crime scene, yellow tape was everywhere. They had the whole block taped off from 40th Street back to 37th Street because he was in a house on 38th street of Greenwood Ave.

We were standing there just in disbelief now what was going through my mind was payback. I was so hurt and angry just full of emotions. I will never forget this moment because GOD saw what was on my mind and what was in my heart. GOD sent this Police Officer to me and he said, "Son I see it in your eyes.

VIOLENCE BEGOT VIOLENCE!" Then he turned around and walked away. After he had said that to me all my emotions I was experiencing, GOD balled into a ball inside of me and the violence was suppressed. The time we got there was around 8:25 pm. So I called my family to let them know what happened. Some showed up and some didn't but we were all full of questions. WHYS? WHATS? We were just clueless. I asked the Officer where he got shot and he replied, "He got shot in the head."

The reason why I asked the Officer is that I was told at this particular time that Aron's Godfather was there and I asked him what led to this. He told me that earlier that day he woke up and saw he missed two phone calls from Aron that morning.

Around 9 am, that morning they got in touch with him and came over to their house, from 9 am to about 2 pm that afternoon, laughing and talking and having a good time. Her name was brought up in the conversation.

Aron's God-Father told him, "Nephew she almost got sons your age. You don't think that one day they going to kill you for their Mother?" Aron turned around and laughed and replied, "They ain't cut like that." So his God-Father explained about three weeks before all this went down that Aron got into it with her so the family was lite-weight mad at Aron.

Also early on in 2021, Aron received a call from a friend saying that a guy wanted to put their hands on her. He goes over there just to make peace about that situation. He gets there and that guy got all into his friend's face, Aron try to break up the argument but the guy tried to hit Aron so he got the best of him. This was suppose to be the Uncle of the family member who shot and killed Aron. His God-Father told me what was told to him was that he was in a rap battle and both parties draw out there guns at the same time but other guy was quicker then Aron so he shot him in the stomach.

This wasn't the truth! Another story was told that Aron had got into an argument with one of the family members over a rap video and

Aron pulled out a gun at one of the family members, the other family pulled their gun out in self-defense and shot Aron. That story wasn't true, either.

We stood out there from 8:25 pm to 1:30 am. All of their family was gone at this time, but our family stood there and I watched our son get zipped up in a black body bag as they was carrying them out of the house into the crime scene SUV. I watched them pull off and when I saw all of that, I burst out in a scream of emotions and anger banging my hand on the back of the trunk of the car, just screaming and crying and saying, “Why? Lord Why?...Why, my only son?”

After I settled myself and got myself together, that's when reality kicked in. WOW! We had to get prepared for a funeral and a little after that the Pastor came up to me and said, "The Lord told me to tell you to give it six months." At that time I didn't understand that my mind was all over the place that night so everyone had left the crime scene about 1:30 am that morning.

LLTG
&$!#%

Rest up

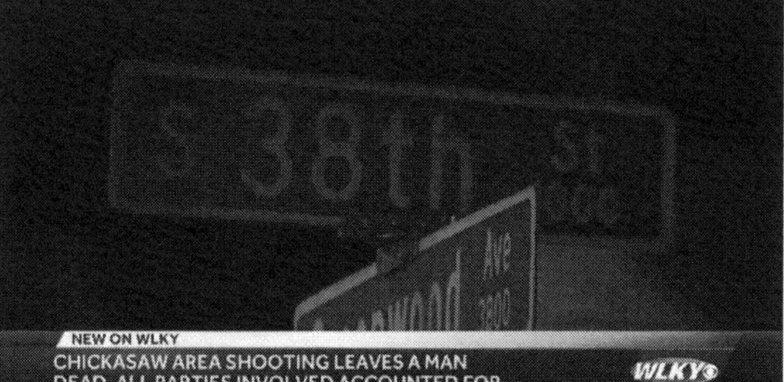
S 38th St
Ave
3800
NEW ON WLKY
CHICKASAW AREA SHOOTING LEAVES A MAN
DEAD, ALL PARTIES INVOLVED ACCOUNTED FOR
WLKY

age 22

Lost to gun violence on August 22, 2021 in Louisville, Kentucky.

LOUISVILLE, Ky. — A deadly weekend has just gotten deadlier as a man was found dead with at least one gunshot wound at a house in the Chickasaw neighborhood Sunday evening, according to Louisville Metro Police.

Officers responded to a call around 7:45 p.m. at a house near the intersection of South 38th St. and Greenwood Avenue. A man was found inside the home and was pronounced dead at the scene.

CHAPTER 19
"DAY OF MOURNING & PREPARATION"

Matthew 5:4
[4] "Blessed [forgiven, refreshed by God's grace] are those who mourn [over their sins and repent], for they will be comforted [when the burden of sin is lifted].

The comfort that Jesus offers to all who mourn with godly sorrow is that the sin that they repent over can come to an end in their lives. Spiritual poverty comes from the conviction of personal sin. Those who seek close fellowship with the Lord mourn over their sin by seeing sin the way God sees it. Those who mourn, by definition, are not happy. Jesus wants His followers to understand that those who experience mourning are not hopeless.

It's August 23, 2021, the next morning talking to the detective and getting different reports. We told them to send his body to Newcomer Funeral Home, the time was about 3 am. The morning came for us to prepare for service from the business perspective. We were full of disbelief and more in shock. When we got there we met up with my wife's spiritual sister and her husband who is close and dear to us and who we can trust because at this point we didn't know who did this to our son. So we didn't trust anyone at this point. While we were in the conference room to set up funeral arrangements, I found out that the insurance I had Aron coverage under said that his coverage was canceled due to his age being 22

The insurance coverage was for ages 0-21. That was not good news so I looked at my wife and said, "What are we going to do?" She replied "Plan B." So we all agreed and continued on the arrangements setting up the Go-Fund-Me account on FB. When we got done the detective called back and said "Why are the names not matching, they need to identify him to make sure that it is their loved one?" We went where his body was and immediately when we all saw it was him my wife took off running in shock.

Her sister chased after her, and her husband and I just stood there looking. The strangest thing was happening, all at the same time the PEACE of GOD was over his body. His peace was so heavy that it dried up our tears we couldn't even cry and His peace gave me the courage to walk over there to look at his body and examine it. When I did I saw five gunshot holes in his head. God revealed to me in a vision right there as I was looking and examining his head; two shots went through the same hole on his right side just a little above his right ear. Two shots that had ricocheted off each other and exited out the top left side of his head and the other had exit out the back of his head close to his left ear and the third shot was when his body hit the ground. His body was lying on his right side so the third shot was on his left cheek and exited out his right temple. This is how he had five holes in his head. So we stepped away and continued to look at him still in shock.

While we were looking at him in silence the PEACE of GOD just continued to hover over his body. He looked like he was breathing; like he was sleeping. There was so much peace GOD preserved his body and his head didn't swell up from gunshot trauma what ever they were trying to do like a closed casket didn't work. We began talking about it amongst each other and we said our last goodbyes to Aron and finished up the business part of the arrangements. We went back home and called family members about what day were the arrangements, but at this point, we didn't trust anybody because the stories of how, when, and what happened were all over the place at this point.

Newcomer
Cremations • Funerals • Receptions

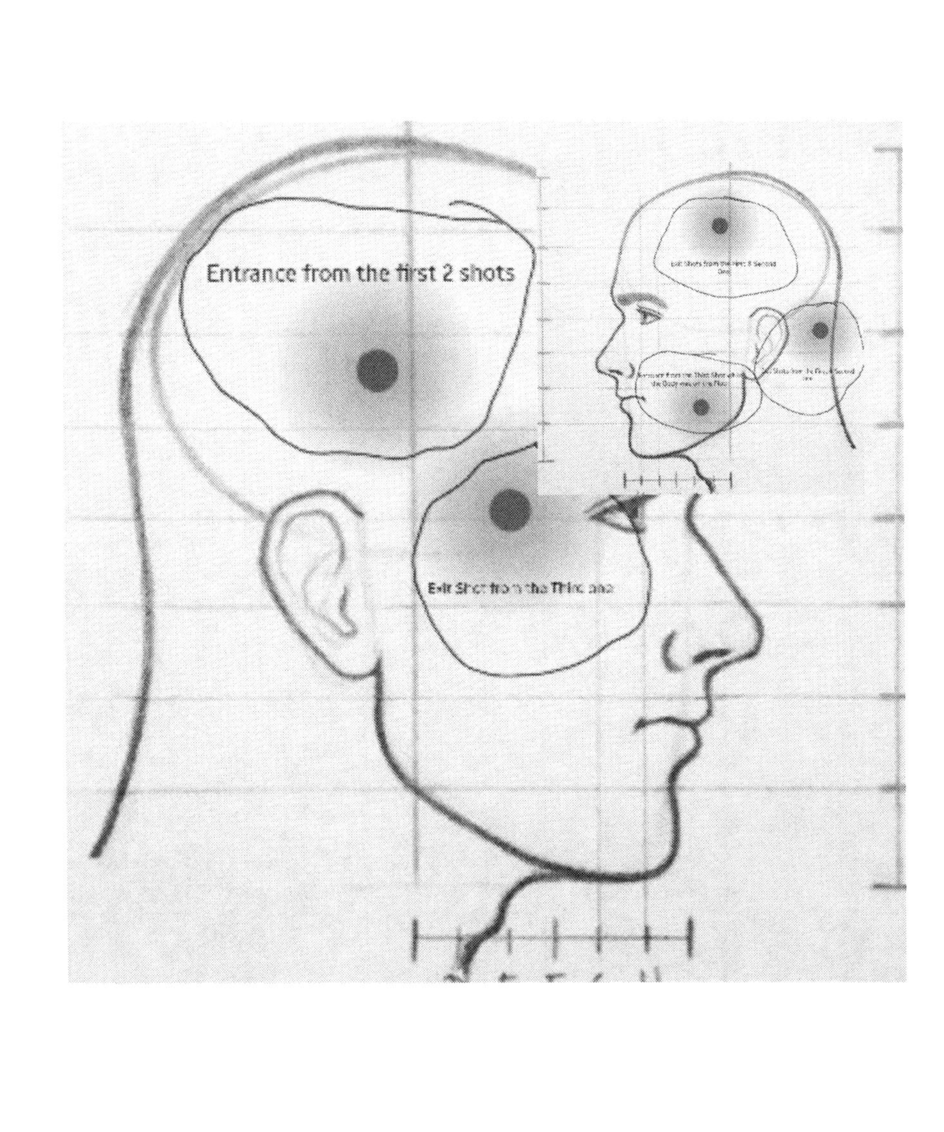
Entrance from the first 2 shots

CHAPTER 20

"GOD REVEALING"

Matthew 7:7-8

[7] " Ask and keep on asking and it will be given to you; seek and keep on seeking and you will find; knock and keep on knocking and the door will be opened to you. [8] For everyone who keeps on asking receives, and he who keeps on seeking finds, and to him who keeps on knocking, it will be opened.

The teaching of ask and receive tells us that we should approach God regularly to ask for our needs. And it also reveals God's heart towards his children; he wants to give good gifts. In this view asking, seeking, and knocking are all metaphors for the act of prayer. In the original language, the terms ask, seek, and knock are/were intended to mean a continuous act versus a one-time act: Ask (and keep asking), and it will be given to you. Seek (and keep seeking), and you will find. Knock (and keep knocking) and the door will be open.

It's Tuesday of that same week August 24, 2021, now I remember being so, so angry at GOD thinking about everything that happened. My mind went back to earlier that year, I remember when Pastor told everyone to write all their loved ones on a sheet of paper and anoint the paper and put it in Matthew 7:7 so we all did that...so I ask God, "Why? Why? That was my only seed on this earth you let this happen to him!, "WHY?" As I was walking around the living room in circles, my phone just blowing up with calls of concern but I didn't care who was calling me at this point.

When I got to the other side of the living room table GOD answered. GOD said to me, "Son you are selfish! What the Lord giveth...the Lord can take it away." I was in complete silence. GOD started explaining, "You know about boxing, right? When a boxer gets hit he falls down but he gets back up right?" I was still silent. GOD showed me a vision of the human body. He showed me the brain and the heart, GOD said to me, "The brain does not give Life....the human heart does.... so while your son was lying there I visited him."

I stood there quietly trying to process everything GOD just told me so I shared it with my wife and we both believed GOD. Our minds went back to Monday when we had that encounter, the PEACE of GOD experience at the Funeral Home over Aron's body. I was encouraged after the visitation from GOD in the living room. So later that week we received two items in the mail that were mailed to us from a friend in Florida. I received a memorial necklace and my wife received a memorial bracelet. We are still trying to be strong in all of this, and still getting phone calls from family members and other people who know Aron about retaliation.

I told them, "NO!" GOD SAID, "NO!" I told them the battle is not ours it's the Lord's and we will leave it in his Hands. Some got mad at me but they received it crying, because after GOD told me he visited Aron, my faith in GOD increased even more after that. All that rage and anger, GOD turned into peace and love and forgiveness. So later on that week on Saturday, I believe it was our 3rd Jurisdictional Women's Convention in Indianapolis, Indiana. Our future-son-law let us use his truck. With Aron on our minds, we trying to press our way there. We got there on Friday night and the next day we were getting ready for the service. No one knew what was going on with us, trying to figure out how in the world we were going to come up with $10,000 before 9/11/21. We went into the service praising GOD and giving him GLORY not even thinking about what just happened trying to focus on GOD.

By the end of the service, word got around to our Bishop when he heard this he stopped everything for this situation and everyone started giving from their heart. From everywhere money was coming this touched our hearts. We both burst out in tears, GOD was showing us he got this.

As we were riding back home from the Women's Convention, we were very encourage. We got home trusting and believing GOD will make a way for Aron's funeral cost. As days went by the people were giving from all different parts of the city, state, and out of town. GOD was performing his mercy right before our eyes. He was letting us know that when you remain FAITHFUL to him, he will do the same for you. This increased our faith in him even more. On September 10th, all of a sudden we get a donation notification WOW! Someone donated the amount we needed and some of it overflowed to where we were able to pay off the Funeral cost and our Bills. "WON'T HE DO IT!! So we praise GOD for that!

WRITE LIKE
MAYA
ROSA
THINK LIKE
GARVEY
BUILD LIKE
MADAM CJ
SPEAK LIKE

WRITE LIKE
MAYA
ROSA

WRITE LIKE
MAYA
ROSA
THINK LIKE
GARVEY
BUILD LIKE
MADAM CJ
SPEAK LIKE
FREDRICK

CHAPTER 21

"9-11-21 GOD DID IT AGAIN"

Hebrews 11:6-7
[6] But without faith it is impossible to [walk with God and] please Him, for whoever comes [near] to God must [necessarily] believe that God exists and that He rewards those who [earnestly and diligently] seek Him. [7] By faith [with confidence in God and His word] Noah, being warned by God about events not yet seen, in reverence prepared an ark for the salvation of his family. By this [act of obedience] he condemned the world and became an heir of the righteousness which comes by faith.

When we trust God, based on what we know of Him, we act according to His will. That is the "faith" which God commands, and which is required to please Him. Prior examples of this kind of faith were Abel and Enoch. Noah, listed here, also exemplifies trusting obedience. The God who rules and reigns over all is the One who rewards those who seek Him. Let us long to seek God and find our reward in Him. To please God, we must believe that God exists.

It's September 10th, 2021. The day before the funeral we were $600 short and didn't know how it was going to come to bury our Son but we didn't give up. While we were there at the Funeral Home two checks dropped into the account that made it $10,000 and more. We were able to get him something to wear and were blessed to pay bills with the overflow.

On 9/11/21 at the Funeral Home, my wife and I were comforting families and real close friends and the Saints. As I was standing next to the casket greeting as they were viewing Aron his biological mother came up with tears...so much hurt in her heart, she was crying out "Our Son! Our Son!"

So as I was comforting her the more she cried harder and the more she would say "Our Son! Our Son !" The more she said "Our Son", I got upset and I asked her "Where are his brothers? Why are they not here?" she responded, "I don't know". I told her "STOP BEING SELFISH!...that was my only child on this earth. You still have two sons that you can save...my seed is in the dirt he ain't coming back... but you still have a chance with your two sons!"

After saying this to her she got quiet and calmed down her emotions. When I look back on her I can tell that what I told her was settling down in her mind. Around this time was the viewing of Aron, his Homegoing Service had not started yet. She stayed around for a little bit longer and went outside for a while. So at this time, a lot of people were very emotional some were upset, and some were calm. Two of his very close friends arrived with their mothers. One of them was there in the house with him and the other one wasn't there when that happened to him.

At that time tension started swelling up in the atmosphere so the one who was there in the house with him crying and was very emotional. Some of the family members had pulled him outside with questions like why and what happened?...at this time I was inside comforting family members and friends. Before service started, I mean that day was very emotional for everyone including my mother looking at her grandson in a casket. She couldn't believe it all, momma was thinking about earlier that year I sent Aron to help momma move into her new place. Aron and some of his friends from Chicago came down to help Aron help my mother and my sister move.

That was something special for momma. That is why my mother was so hurt because out of all her grandchildren, Aron was something special to her. I believe because he being my only child was special. The homegoing service has now started everyone outside came in but Aron's mother and her sister (his auntie) had left, they didn't stay for service. I understood because it was too much for her, a very emotional situation. Everything was Beautiful, words of encouragement and the message was powerful.

The possessional was gathering around outside family and friends were taking pictures together. The repass was at the church after the burial so we all got to the grave site to pay our last respects to my son. After that, some left heading to the church some of us stayed to watch him being put in the ground and take his rest. In of him, I was the first to throw dirt on top of his casket and those who were there also did the same.

After that, the rest of us headed to the church for the repass meal. Two of his close friends came and the one who was there in the house with him told me what had happened, what he witnessed that fatal day. His story was that he was in the other room with a female when all of a sudden he heard Aron arguing with someone. It got quiet for a moment...then he heard three shots and he ran where he heard the three shots. He said he looked down and Aron was lying there and blood was everywhere. He said Aron's body was moving (shaking), and he said he looked for Aron's gun but didn't find it on him. He said that he was so emotional that he went downstairs and walked around in circles then walked back upstairs and left before the Police came. I told him I heard something different and I told him, and he replied "That ain't true Aron was innocent he didn't come over there on BS mode, Aron was chilled and lay back. Aron didn't start anything they started with him!" So I ask him "so why didn't you tell the Police" he couldn't answer that question because of fear I believe.

Afterward, while we were eating the Lord began to use me to minister to those young men and shared what GOD revealed to me concerning them...they received it...but after that, I began to put two and two together thinking about everything that I heard concerning what happened to our son Aron on that fatal day, by definition, not being happy. Jesus wants His followers to understand that those who experience mourning are not hopeless.

CHAPTER 22
"GOD PROVEN PROOF"

Romans 1:18-20

[18] For [God does not overlook sin and] the wrath of God is revealed from heaven against all ungodliness and unrighteousness of men who in their wickedness suppress and stifle the truth, [19] because that which is known about God is evident within them [in their inner consciousness], for God made it evident to them. [20] For ever since the creation of the world His invisible attributes, His eternal power and divine nature, have been clearly seen, being understood through His workmanship [all His creation, the wonderful things that He has made], so that they [who fail to believe and trust in Him] are without excuse and without defense.

Those who live unrighteous lives, whether believers or nonbelievers, will experience the wrath of God. The wrath of God here is God giving us over to the natural consequences of our choices. God has given everyone knowledge of right and wrong, giving no one an excuse. No one likes to talk about the wrath of God, particularly if it is thought of in a relationship about ourselves. But if we have to think about it, as the study of these verses forces us to do so, we find ourselves reacting generally in one of two ways. Either (1) we argue that wrath is somehow unworthy of God, a blotch on His character, and therefore a mistaken notion that should be abandoned at once by all right-thinking people; or (2) we reply by denying that we merit God's wrath, that we don't deserve it. This second reaction is the more serious of the two.

So it is the one Paul tackles in the development of his argument for the need we all have for the Christian gospel. It's the first month and a couple of days after we buried our son, Aron. I visited Aron's resting place, paying my respects.

On October 17, 2021, we received mail, it was Aron's Death Certificate. We opened the mail and began to examine it. We read the shooting happened at (19:47 Military time), the next thing we looked at was the time of death was (20:04 Military time) and the last thing we looked at was how long he was alive, it said 17 minutes which meant his heart was beating for 17 minutes.

As I was looking at the death certificate the Holy Ghost quickened, brought back to my mind that when we were at the Funeral Home viewing his body I remembered the PEACE of GOD was in the room. The second time He quickened my mind was the next day when I was pacing around the living room table when GOD spoke to me and showed me a vision in my mind about what took place in that house on that fatal night...BOOM! That is when GOD showed me what he did in those 17 minutes he visited Aron while his heart was beating.

The more I understood the more wisdom and knowledge of God were pouring into me all at the same time. So I rejoice with excitement and enthusiasm. GOD is so so so GOOD because I was so concerned and angry towards GOD about his soul and his well-being. So after seeing GOD's evidence, I repented to GOD and asked him for forgiveness because I believe without a shadow of a doubt that GOD visited our son and gave him one more chance before his heart stopped beating, in 17minutes he was SAVED our Son on his Death Bed. WOW! "AIN'T GOD AMAZING!" So GOD did it again. Now the word hit me all of a sudden I began to grieve and the reality of it hit me so I began crying, and weeping hard at work, thank God it was on a Friday. I called my wife and said to her, "I want to get away I need to go out of town or do something?" She replied, "Where do you want to go?"

I answered "NFL Hall of Fame in Canton, Ohio."
She replied, "Ok the bills are paid we got money saved so we good...you sure you want to leave this late?"
I answered, "Yes, I'm ready."
When I got off work we packed some clothes, filled the car up with gas, and hit the road.

RO FOOTBALL
HALL OF FAME
CANTON, OHIO

Heinz
Field

Steelers

ARON TRAYNOR
SNORDON
FEB 11, 1999–AUG 22, 2021

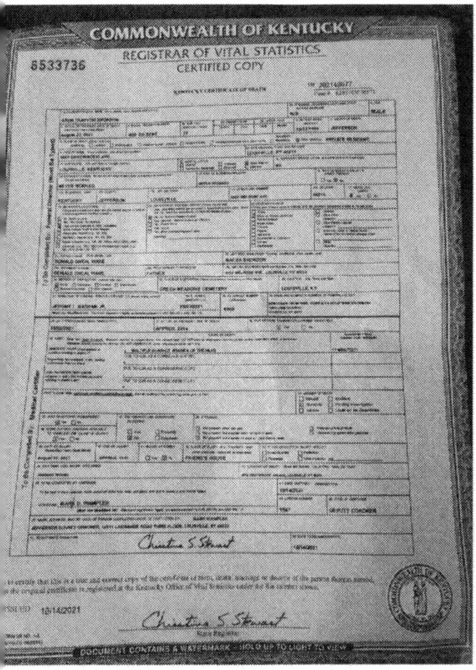

COMMONWEALTH OF KENTUCKY

REGISTRAR OF VITAL STATISTICS

6533736

CERTIFIED COPY

Christina S. Stewart

10/14/2021

Christina S. Stewart

DOCUMENT CONTAINS A WATERMARK - HOLD UP TO LIGHT TO VIEW

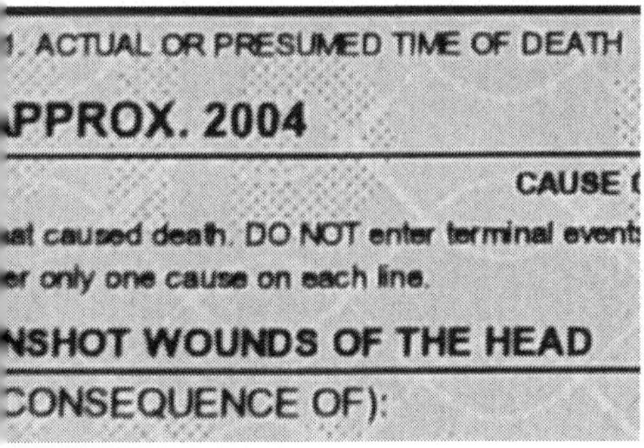

1. ACTUAL OR PRESUMED TIME OF DEATH

APPROX. 2004

CAUSE

at caused death. DO NOT enter terminal events

er only one cause on each line.

NSHOT WOUNDS OF THE HEAD

CONSEQUENCE OF):

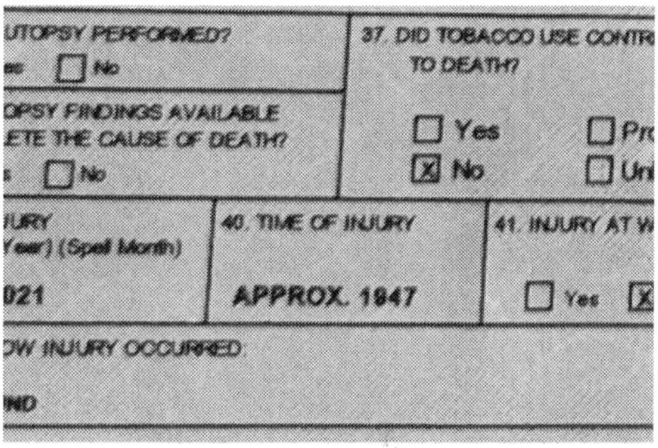

UTOPSY PERFORMED?

es ☐ No

OPSY FINDINGS AVAILABLE
ETE THE CAUSE OF DEATH?

s ☐ No

37. DID TOBACCO USE CONTR
TO DEATH?

☐ Yes ☐ Pr
☒ No ☐ Un

JURY
Year) (Spell Month)

021

40. TIME OF INJURY

APPROX. 1947

41. INJURY AT W

☐ Yes ☒

OW INJURY OCCURRED:

ND

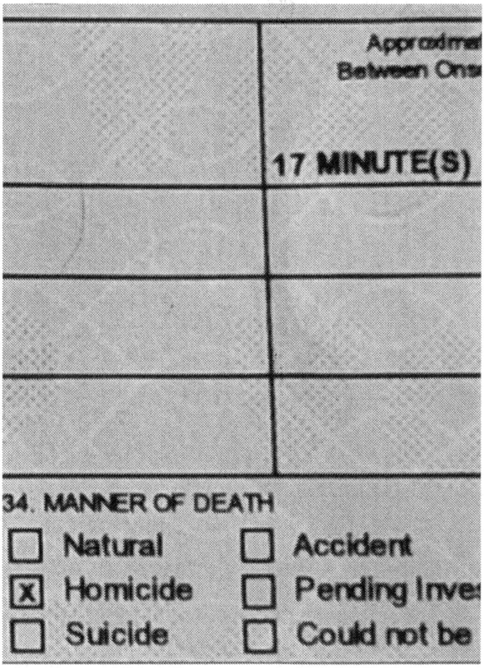

Approxima
Between Ons

17 MINUTE(S)

34. MANNER OF DEATH

☐ Natural ☐ Accident
☒ Homicide ☐ Pending Inves
☐ Suicide ☐ Could not be

CHAPTER 23
"GOD'S APPROVAL"

Proverbs 24:16-18
[16] For a righteous man falls seven times, and rises again, But the wicked stumble in times of disaster and collapse. [17] Do not rejoice and gloat when your enemy falls, And do not let your heart be glad [in self-righteousness] when he stumbles, [18] Or the Lord will see your gloating and be displeased, And turn His anger away from your enemy.

Whether the "righteous fall seven times" or as a figurative meaning representing many times, the promise is true, "they will rise again." With God's care, the upright persevere through hard times, knowing God's plan is for good, and if it's not good yet, it's in process. Here, Solomon expresses confidence that godly people can recover from setbacks. Those who do evil fall when struck by adversity. God watches how you treat your enemies. If you are happy when bad things happen to them, He will help them and possibly punish you. God protects His children by punishing their enemies, but He will end that punishment if He sees you gloating.

It's now the year 2022 from the time of Aron's death to now, within these six months, many things happened. One week after we buried our son the Lord woke my wife up in the middle of the night and told her to anoint the grounds around our house and to anoint the house. She did as God told her not knowing why. That following Sunday, we were in the house with our granddaughters having a great time just getting home from church.

Then we started watching Michael Jackson on TV and all of a sudden, we heard 11 loud gunshots. It was so loud that we thought they were on our front porch. It shook and paralyzed us. As soon as the gunshots were over we immediately ran outside to check. Come to find out, our neighbor saw everything and it scared him enough to where he had to grab his gun, pointed the gun, and was nearly about to shoot. Everything happened so quickly but everything seemed to move slowly. It felt like the shooting lasted forever. This wasn't the first time. Our neighbor's next door house got shot up more than two times. The instructions God had given my wife to do all came together. It dawned on us, that this is why the Lord told my wife to anoint the grounds around the house. We believed that it might have been for us but God guided the bullets somewhere else. God truly protected us.

In January 2022, I was diagnosed with COVID-19 and was out of work for a week, my wife took good care of me. From the time of Aron's death to this point my wife had scheduled a vacation for herself to clear her head, she went back home for two weeks and I was home by myself. I was seeking the Lord concerning everything and my marriage in these two weeks, I waited for GOD to answer. On the last day of my wife's vacation, she was on her way back home and I was at work. That Monday while I was on my forklift ready to load up my container the Lord spoke to me and said "Go and do whatever it takes to make her happy." So I immediately got happy and called my wife and told her what the Lord said she responded, "HALLELUJAH! that is confirmation from GOD, yes that was Him talking to you". We begin to make plans to move out of Louisville, Kentucky. I let my family know some of them understood and some didn't like it. My mother was one of them who didn't like it, she had her own opinion concerning the move. I responded to momma "I have to do what GOD said to us and it will be a fresh start for us, starting over!" Of course, momma got into her feelings, mom got upset and hung up the phone.

Our moving date was in the last week of June 2022. As we were getting into the preparation of moving, one day the Lord spoke to my wife and said to her to tell me that "I will be a Father of many young in Christ", and that you should write a Book of Aron...so I received it and took heed to what God told my wife. We ate out with Pastor Porter & and First Lady Porter at a breakfast restaurant called "First Watch" off Bardstown Road in Louisville, Kentucky.

After eating and fellowshipping we were all standing outside of the restaurant, I was talking to Pastor Porter and he said to me "Lord said to me to tell you, "have you thought about Mentorship for the Youth?" I replied "No", then he asked, "Have you thought about writing a Book?"

I replied, "WOW! My wife said the same thing and yes I thought about writing a book about him. This was confirmation".

We were coming up with ideas for the name of the book. So when we got home the Lord spoke to me and said, "Name the Book 22 YEARS IN 17 MINUTES" I replied "Why?" God responded, "22 YEARS REPRESENTS his life on earth and the 17 MINUTES represents the moment of time I gave him to visit me...it's not always people I save in the church, sometimes it's on their death bed." I didn't respond because I was so full of "Aww" so the Lord continued to talk to me, and took me to Proverbs 24:16-18:

"[16] For a righteous man falls seven times, and rises again, But the wicked stumble in time of disaster and collapse.

[17] Do not rejoice and gloat when your enemy falls, And do not let your heart be glad [in self-righteousness] when he stumbles,

[18] Or the Lord will see your gloating and be displeased, And turn His anger away, from your enemy." So the LORD explains what this means he said to me.

"When you hear of things happening do not celebrate because if you do I will let your enemies know where you are. Forgive them and pray for them." Around this time it was six months later after Aron got murder. Just like the Lord told our pastor to tell me the day of that crime scene.

Shortly after this, I began hearing things about what truly happened on the day of that crime scene. Information was leaking out like puzzle pieces. I had to put all this information together and it began to make sense. The sources of the information said that "this family was mad at Aron for an argument that took place between him and the female friend of that home, happened about three weeks before the shooting. The female friend of that home finally got in touch with Aron with a cellphone call on August 22, 2021, earlier that day she asked him, "Do you still want your Hair done?" Aron replied, "Yeah." Sources said, that it was a setup to kill Aron. Also it was said that Aron did not go over there to hurt anyone it was said that he arrived to get his hair done, take a shower, and go back to his God-Father's home.

This was the plan but Aron never made it back and he didn't see this coming, it was said that while Aron was in the shower a family member of the female had come over there while Aron was getting dressed (putting on changing Clothes).

This family member was upset at Aron over that argument with the female three weeks before all this happened. After Aron put his clothes on he then asked the female "Can you cook that Steak for me?" she replied: "Sure", the family member of the female replied to her, "MAN DON'T FIX THAT NIGGER S#$%!" So Aron replied to him and the argument started between Aron and him. Words were said back and forth so it was said that the guy wanted to fight Aron outside and other family members were also at home at the time the argument happened.

Sources say that as they were exiting the home Aron and the guy were arguing.

They were the last two coming out of the house, as Aron got close to the door the guy that was walking behind him sidestepped Aron on his right side, pointed the gun at his head, and shot him twice. As Aron's body dropped and fell on his right side on the ground his body was shaking. Sources said that he shot Aron the 3rd time on the left side of his face on his cheek after this they waited to call the Police. This gave them time to stage this as a self-defense act. Within these six months, GOD told me that I would hear things about what happened to Aron, a lie can only go so far before the truth starts leaking out. This happened in March, four months before moving when God told me this.

[16] For a righteous man falls seven times, and rises again, But the wicked stumble in time of disaster and collapse. [17] Do not rejoice and gloat when your enemy falls, And do not let your heart be glad [in self-righteousness] when he stumbles, [18] Or the Lord will see your gloating and be displeased, And turn His anger away from your enemy.

Proverbs 24:16-18 AMP

AFFORDABLE
COVERAGE
LAWVILLE
MORRIS' DELI
& CATERING
Lite

CHAPTER 24
"GOD'S PREPARATION"

Lamentations 3:31-33
[31] For the Lord will not reject forever, [32] For if He causes grief, Then He will have compassion According to His abundant lovingkindness and tender mercy. [33] For He does not afflict willingly and from His heart Or grieve the children of men.

God will not abandon people forever, and even when he causes grief, he will also show compassion because of his unfailing love. The passage also suggests that God does not intentionally cause people pain or sorrow. God's compassions fail not; of this, we have fresh mercies every morning. Portions on earth are perishing things, but God is a portion forever. It is our duty and will be our comfort and satisfaction, to hope and quietly wait for the salvation of the Lord. So it's March 24, 2022, and momma's birthday fell on our work day. After we worked we stopped by momma's house with gifts and a Birthday Cake to cheer her up. Momma was turning 75 years old, I asked momma, "What's wrong?" She replied, "I don't feel so good..."My toe is hurting" so I asked, "Why?" She explained why it was hurting, she had clipped her toenail too close and cut the skin and it was getting infected. She was a little grouchy that day but we understood.

Between March and April, momma had scheduled surgery on April 14th for the artery in her right leg. This was a couple of weeks after her birthday. One day my wife and I were talking about the moving date.

She said that the Lord laid it on her heart to change the moving date from June 24th to July 24th she didn't know why but we believed GOD. We didn't understand why GOD changed it, but we stuck with the change. Momma's surgery was successful, they also cleaned the infected area of her right toe so she was able to come home the same day.

So between April and June, momma was healing from surgery and started to feel better. She started to go back to church and became active singing in the Choir again. She started going back to bible study, etc. One day momma and I were talking on the phone about everything and momma said, "I'm glad you are moving out of this city, you need it and maybe you can take your brother too. I am worried about him" I replied, "Yeah he needs to it might be good for him" so we both started laughing. I told momma about the plan of giving our trampoline to my sister's grandchildren and our barbecue grill. Momma was so excited she responded, "WOW! that's good, I'm looking forward to that OH WOW! Your sister is going to be happy about this!" I also told momma that GOD told us to "Start over fresh" momma responded, "I believe that was GOD", as we were prepping up to make our new move in the month of June, momma began to start feeling bad again at this point no one didn't know why.

On Father's Day June 19, 2022, we got up early on that day and got dressed to go to our Son's resting place (graveyard site). Momma called and asked if we could pick her up and take her to the store, I got upset because someone was there with a car. We went and paid our respects afterward we went and picked up momma and took her to Kroger. When we got there I noticed how momma was slowly walking. When we got into the store she was out of breath and getting tired. My wife and I told momma to sit down and rest. We got her list and did her shopping for her. After we got done with the groceries my wife and momma were having a good conversation amongst themselves.

We got to the car and put the groceries in. As we were leaving momma just burst out in tears saying, "Why did they do that to my grandson like that, why!"....."Aron didn't deserve that!" Momma had been grieving ever since Aron got murdered. I responded, "Momma everything is going to be alright, God got Aron he told me he did." Momma responded, "I'm upset about it"...I responded, "Momma God is in control, I had to listen to GOD...GOD told me in his Word". Momma eventually calmed down. We got momma home, and she was excited about cooking a Father's Day meal even though she was feeling bad. She still cooked and we stayed around for a little bit and then we left.

The day after Father's Day, momma's sickness was getting worse in and out of the restroom all day. On Tuesday I didn't get a phone call, momma normally calls me but this day she didn't. I was concerned and I called momma's phone. My little brother answered her phone and I asked, "Where is momma?" he responded, "Lying down." I asked him to "go check on her!"...he checked on her, and said, "Momma good, she's ok, she been sleeping all day." I responded, "Oh....ok" and I got off the phone with him. It's Wednesday I was getting off work and received a phone call from my sister saying, "Momma ain't doing good we call the ambulance, Momma got to go to the Hospital something ain't right with her" I responded: "Ok on my way!" I stop by my house, told my wife what was going on and I'm heading over momma. My wife responded, "Ok, I'm praying for her." I said "Ok"... I got to my sister's house (Momma and my sister were living together).

The ambulance arrived and the paramedic was in the house. I go in and I look at momma she looked very, very weak, she barely could stand up. I helped them get her on the stretcher, they put her in the ambulance and I followed them to the hospital. When we got to the ER (Emergency Room) it was overcrowded. They had her room out in the hallway with a curtain around her. Momma was having some type of attack within her body, it was off and on.

Momma thought she was having a heart attack because of the pain she was having. She would lay back down for about 10 minutes, then popped back up, this was going on for about 30 minutes. The last time she popped back up, she turned and looked at me and said, "Donald I'm so tired... I'm so so so tired", then she lay back down.

I was praying the entire time I was at the hospital. When she lay back down I walked away and began to cry because when she said that to me I knew momma wasn't going to make it out of the hospital this time. It was only me there at the hospital nobody but me, so I got angry and I asked God, "Why me Lord...why is it always me here by myself with momma every time she gets sick?" GOD answered me, and said, "Why not YOU!"...so my reply was, "Yes Lord, I understand, I am a man of God that is why you have me here with her to help her get through." God gave me peace of mind and to be STRONG. So hours went by and they finally got her into a room. At this time momma was fighting to live because she knew her time was winding up so at this point I got in my flesh and got upset at the RN's nurses and I asked, "WHAT IS Y'ALL DOING!...AIN'T THIS WHAT Y'ALL WENT TO SCHOOL FOR!...IF THIS WAS YOUR MOTHER WANT Y'ALL TRY TO SAVE HER! SO HELP HER!...AIN'T THIS WHAT THEY PAY Y'ALL FOR!...SO DO Y'ALL JOB!" After I said that the RN's nurses started working on her. I went and sat in the waiting room area and began to cry still seeing that frightening look on my mother's face of fear.

Later on, the doctor came and told me my mother's report shows that she became Septic (Bacteria throughout her blood system in her entire body). They told me her only chance of living was to put her on a dialysis machine but if her Heart was not strong enough, she might not survive. I called my wife and I asked her what I should do, she replied "Do it...it might be her only chance. I called my sister and told her she also agreed. All of this happened early Wednesday morning so later on I went home, got some rest, and went back and forth to the Hospital.

On Thursday family and the Saints were coming, praying and spending time with her. I had spent the night that Thursday and early Friday morning my two younger brothers and my sister and niece came together so we spent time together with her...later they all left but I stayed. I fell asleep and was in a deep sleep, my mother came and whispered in my ear "Baby go home get you some rest and spend time with your wife I will be alright", I woke up immediately. It felt like I was asleep for about 8 hours but only 10 minutes. I got up and went to her room because of what I had experienced.

I thought she had gotten up out of bed and whispered that in my ear because I heard her voice. I saw her lying there and I pondered on it for a while. I did just as she told me to do. It's about 10:45 pm on Friday night, my phone rings I answered, and the lady on the other end says, "This is the nurse at the hospital where your mom is at. You need to get here A.S.A.P! Your mom's heart rate is doing some weird stuff call your family and let them know", I responded, "On my Way! So I called family and friends as we where heading to the hospital the LORD spoke to me with urgency and said, "When you get there to her room, grab her hand, PRAY immediately so we got there and I did exactly as the LORD told me. I began to pray in the spirit, the prayer of repentance, at this moment it was just my wife, niece, and me in the room.

As I was praying, her heart rate was counting down from 80% to 0%. So before it got to 0% I completed the prayer of repentance. So the LORD began to lead me into telling her encouragement so I knew in my heart that this was it. After the encouragement she looked at me, she looked at my wife, and then her Granddaughter (My niece) saying her goodbye with her eyes. She was moving her mouth talking to us, and after that, she gave up the ghost in peace. (My mother went into the hospital earlier that week on Tuesday night, and on Friday night June 24, 2022, at 11:30 pm she made her transition). Afterward, the LORD's presence came into that room to comfort us and dried away everyone's tears, because of GOD's presence.

The family began to show up at the hospital and everyone started gathering in the room. I turned around and looked at my wife and said "So the doctor was praying with us too?"

My Wife responded, "No, there was no doctor standing by me...it was just the three of us", I replied, "I seen someone standing in all white between you and my niece like a doctor." She responded, "No there was no one else." I knew after that the LORD came and approved that prayer for momma.

The next day my little brother had spent the night over at our house. That morning everything hit all at once I began weeping (Crying so hard) saying, "Momma! Momma! I'm so, so sorry Momma!" My wife and my little brother were consoling me by saying "It wasn't your fault this was GOD's doing and His decision." I begin to calm down, I got myself together and began praying and waiting patiently on the Lord's direction in preparing for home going service for my mother. So the next day I was thinking of certain ones who could preach my mother's eulogy. The LORD spoke to me, "No...why not YOU!" The LORD gave me a Word to preach that day. I began to prepare myself by studying, praying, and fasting for the service.

CHAPTER 25
"FRESH START NEW CHAPTER"

Isaiah 43:18-19
[18] "Do not remember the former things, Or ponder the things of the past. [19] Listen carefully, I am about to do a new thing, Now it will spring forth; Will you not be aware of it? I will even put a road in the wilderness, rivers in the desert.

God is always looking ahead, making minor course adjustments here and there so that everything He ever prophesied about through His people and recorded our past failures, brokenness, and pain no longer define us, condemn us, or rule over us. We are completely new creations and we have a new Spirit living in The Spirit compels us to view our experience of God's grace in the past as a springboard so that we view neither present nor future with fear but with expectation.

On Thursday, June 30, 2022, was our dear beloved Mother Mary Delane Patterson, Homegoing Service. The LORD had prepared my heart and mind for this day, it was a bitter and sweet day. All my brothers and sisters, family, friends, and the Saints came to show their support and Love. I was nervous because this was my first eulogy, especially for my mother. The more I was thinking about it the more the LORD was giving me strength physically and spiritually. The service starts and I'm sitting there listening to everyone who came up front to share their moments and memories with momma. Now it's PREACHING TIME!

I got up and all of a sudden, "To God be the Glory." A powerful unction came from my belly as soon as I opened my mouth, BOOM! God began to use me for his Glory. I Preached like it was no tomorrow. The Message the LORD gave me was "Farewell, Never Good Bye!" Scriptures were John 3:16-19, John 14:1-4, and Revelation 21:4, 5. I remember earlier in my ministry the LORD told me, "Open your mouth and I will speak right through you." I trusted in the Lord that Day and the GLORY of GOD came in that service, it was awesome. The message was about 30 minutes long, I felt great that day.

The next day we began our preparation for moving to Florida because the LORD moved our moving day from June 24, 2022, to July 24, 2022. The LORD revealed this to my wife months earlier but we didn't understand then until after momma passed on June 24, 2022. See GOD doesn't make any mistakes. We gave things away, and people were buying items from us. On the 4th of July, we had our family get-together and it was nothing but all love. We were having a great time, lighting fireworks.

From July 4th to July 24th was hump time, getting rid of things, and selling items it was very hard but GOD was making ways for us. As this was going on the LORD spoke to both of us and said "New Blessings New Beginnings a FRESH START!" So were encouraged in the Spirit. The week before our moving date we both visited family and friends saying our farewells to our co-workers and saints at church, everyone was sad we were leaving Louisville.

I remember my momma's response when we first told her we decided to move to Florida. She was upset but on Father's Day, days before she passed, momma was encouraging us to move out of the city, I will never forget the conversations we had with her. My wife said to her "Yeah maybe we can fly you down so you can meet my Mom & Dad", momma responded, "That sounds good and all but I don't think I'm going to make it that way I have been feeling lately that God might call me home this year."

So momma knew but didn't know when and after that conversations when we were done grocery shopping we were on our way taking momma back home momma was sitting in the back seat and all of a sudden she broke down crying thinking about Aron her Grandson she said "Why they had to do him like that" so I calm her down cheered her up I knew then GOD was up to something. As we were packing up everything, all these thoughts and memories were on my mind before we hit the road to start on our new journey in life, a new chapter, turning a new page in our life, moving just a month after momma's burial. Our daughter and grandchildren stayed to send us off, we hugged and cried and loved on each other. Suddenly it started raining we hurried and packed up, filled up on gas, and hit the road saying "FAREWELL FAREWELL LOUISVILLE!"

Homegoing Celebration
For
Mary Delean Patterson

SUNRISE
March 24, 1947

SUNSET
June 24, 2022

Thursday, June 30, 2022
12:00 P.M.
Hathaway & Clark Funeral Home, Inc.
2718 Virginia Avenue
Louisville, Kentucky 40211

Pastor Brodrick Smith, Sr., Officiating
Breathing New Life Ministries

Don't cry because it's over. Smile because it happened. Perhaps they are not stars but rather openings in heaven where the love of our lost ones pours through and shines down upon us to let us know they are happy. They that love beyond the world cannot be separated by it. Death cannot kill what never dies.

What does the celebration of life mean?

A celebration of life is an opportunity for family and friends to pay tribute to a loved one who has recently passed away. It lets people say goodbye and honor their loved one's legacy in a uniquely personal way. Celebrations of life are often more flexible and creative than funerals, and they can be a meaningful way to say goodbye and honor the deceased's legacy. They can be held at any location, such as a restaurant, reception hall, or the deceased's home, and can include activities like sharing memories, listening to music, or adding refreshments. Mourners are often encouraged to share positive stories about the deceased's life, such as their passions, family, and positive traits. Celebrations of life can be arranged by friends, family, or clergy, and there's no need to hire an official event planner. When planning a celebration of life, it's important to consider the guests' emotional needs and the unique personality and lifestyle of the deceased.

~These pictures were taken one year after
September 11, 2022, ~

In Loving Memory
Aron Trayvon Snordon
February 11, 1999 - August 22, 2021

MICHAEL JORDAN
COME FLY WITH ME
AIR

First, and foremost I want to give honor to God and his Son Jesus who is the head of my life. This is the story of my beloved son Aron Trayvon Snordon "A.T.S," whose life ended in such tragic circumstances. Three gunshots to his head at the age of "22" years old. He was so passionate about life. He lived in a world of great influence by his peers, among wolves and sheep clothing, people he called friends, family, and brothers but eventually one day betrayed him.

So I share his story to let the world know that the devil is out to "STEAL, KILL, & to DESTROY." That is his mission! Those three are the objectives. Listen, parents! WARNING always comes before destruction. As you raise your child or children watch and pray for the Wisdom of God And especially for new parents Always put your child or children before the Lord at all times. I share this story to share my testimony of a father-and-son relationship. Through the good times and bad times and the relationship with GOD. Listen and take heed to the warning signs from GOD in your child or children because the bible tells us as parents in Proverbs 22:6. Train up a child in the way he should go [teaching him to seek God's wisdom and will for his abilities and talents], Even when he is old he will not depart from it. So if you as parents follow GOD'S instructions, God will guide you through good and the bad. Having a relationship with GOD is so very important in the world we are living in. So I hope that this book inspires and encourages you in LIFE.

Gun-related violence is violence committed with the use of a firearm. Gun-related violence may or may not be considered criminal. Criminal violence includes homicide, assault with a deadly weapon, and suicide, or attempted suicide, depending on jurisdiction.

The Bible doesn't mention "gun control" because it was written before guns were invented, but it does contain many accounts of weapons and violence. Some say the Bible's views on gun control include: ***Violence should be a last resort.***

Violence is prohibited if it's in revenge, vigilante justice, or disproportionate to the crime. Proverbs 3:31 says, "Do not envy a violent man or choose any of his ways."

Self-defense

Luke 22:35-38 mentions carrying a weapon for self-defense in a positive light. However, Jesus also said, "All who draw the sword will die by the sword" to Peter when Peter tried to defend Jesus against a mob.

Peacemakers

Christians should be known as peacemakers, and Micah 4:3 says that God is teaching people to "beat their swords into plowshares and their spears into pruning shears."

Personal conviction

Some say that using guns is a matter of personal conviction and that there's nothing wrong with protecting oneself or loved ones, even if it involves weapons.

18

Aron Trayon Snordon
Feb. 11, 1999 8 Lbs. 12 Oz.

Aron T. Snordon

February 11, 1999

August 22, 2021

Mary D. Patterson

March 24, 1947

June 24, 2022

Tracy R. Ware (Jones)

June 12, 1971

October 31, 2023

Made in the USA
Columbia, SC
07 June 2025